The Book of Revelation as a Drama

ROLAND ENGLAND

WESTBOW
P R E S S®
A DIVISION OF THOMAS NELSON
& ZONDERVAN

WestBow Press books may be ordered through booksellers or by contacting:

WestBow Press
A Division of Thomas Nelson & Zondervan
1663 Liberty Drive
Bloomington, IN 47403
www.westbowpress.com
844-714-3454

ISBN: 978-1-6642-1085-1 (sc)
ISBN: 978-1-6642-1084-4 (hc)
ISBN: 978-1-6642-1086-8 (e)

Library of Congress Control Number: 2020921457

Print information available on the last page.

WestBow Press rev. date: 11/24/2020

To Nancy, the love of my life, my sweet
and charming wife of fifty-four years, whose
partnership in the sweetest thing I know on earth

CONTENTS

PREFACE

My first memories of Revelation come from a high school-age Sunday school class in the late 1950s at Emmanuel Reformed Church, Fishers Hill, Virginia. The teacher, my great-aunt Bessie Keller, taught from what I now call the Hal Lindsey School of Biblical Interpretation. (Lindsey later wrote *The Late Great Planet Earth*.) In a lecture format to high schoolers, week after week, Aunt Bess went on and on about the beasts of Revelation. Essentially this all went in one ear and out the other.

Through early adulthood, I read the Bible and took my faith seriously, but I don't recall doing any study in Revelation. Then at age twenty-eight, I entered college under the GI bill. I majored in Bible at Eastern Mennonite College (now Eastern Mennonite University) in Harrisonburg, Virginia. After college, I moved with my wife, Nancy, and young son, James, to Richmond, where I attended Union Theological Seminary (now Union Presbyterian Seminary). At Union from 1972 to 1975, my professors included Dr. John Bright, professor of Old Testament, and Dr. Mathias Rissi, professor of New Testament, two world-renowned Old and New Testament scholars. Professor Rissi was known for his studies in Revelation and the gospel of John.

From Aunt Bessie Keller to Professor Mathias Rissi, what a journey! Yet each one, in their own way, was a faithful disciple of Jesus Christ teaching from the word of God. I gradually became more interested in Revelation over my forty-five years as a pastor. In 2017, I spent a year studying Revelation and preaching from it each Sunday.

As early as 2004, a seed was planted for my writing this book on Revelation. At the time, Rev. Dennis Campbell and I were both pastors working full time as security guards on a federal government contract. Dennis wrote a book on Revelation in defense of a post-millennial point of view. His book, *He Shall Reign*, is listed in the bibliography. Keller, Rissi, and Campbell are numbered among countless Christians fascinated with Revelation. I am adding another voice to this conversation, *Worthy is the Lamb: The Book of Revelation as a Drama*.

The endnotes indicate some authors on which this work depends. However, my reliance on the works of others goes far beyond these notes. As time passes, it becomes harder to identify some sources. I also depend on multiple sources shared among many Revelation scholars.

The scriptural text of Revelation included in this book represents my translation, referencing the Greek text published by United Bible Societies, the New American Standard Bible published by the Lockman Foundation, and the English Standard Version published by Crossway. Like those two English translations, this is essentially a literal word-for-word translation, which closely follows the Greek text. It also follows the format of the Greek text where verses are centered on the page to indicate poems and hymns. Any scripture included in addition to Revelation is from the New American Standard Bible.

I acknowledge the valuable assistance of my brother, Russell England, for his help in editing early copies of the manuscript.

The stained-glass window on the front cover is based on John 19:5. Jesus then came out, wearing the crown of thorns and the purple robe. Pilate said to them, "Behold the Man!"

The stained-glass window in the door on the back cover depicts Revelation 3:20. "Look, I stand at the door and knock; if anyone hears my voice and opens the door, I will come in and we will dine with each other."

These are two of the seventeen stained-glass windows I crafted for our Church. The door, with the window of Jesus knocking, was built by Howard Shawn Hodges. The faces of Jesus were painted by Barbra Quinn.

AN OUTLINE OF THE DRAMA

INTRODUCTION

This book on Revelation follows two basic principles: scripture is to be interpreted in its own historical context and is to be interpreted by other holy scripture. Revelation is a letter addressed to seven first-century churches and includes a personal message for each one. These are actual, historical churches, each one urged to remain faithful to Jesus at the cost of their own lives. Seven is a symbolic number for wholeness or completeness. For example, look at the seven days of creation (Genesis 1:1–2:2). Seven churches represent all the churches—past, present, and future.

Revelation is Christian prophesy, with many similarities to the Hebrew prophets of the Old Testament. It's a prophetic message for believers in the first-century AD. Prophesy may foretell the future, but it may also tell forth (or explain) the meaning of events occurring during the prophet's lifetime. The author writes about what must soon take place (1:1) and says the time is near (1:3). He writes from an understanding of a first-century worldview that divides time into two ages: this age and the age to come. He tells forth the meaning of events occurring during his own lifetime as he looks ahead to the expected age to come. Revelation's larger message speaks to all churches throughout history and remains vitally important to us today.

Revelation is also apocalyptic literature. Apocalypse is the English form of the Greek word translated as Revelation. It means the unveiling of what is hidden. This book's purpose is to unveil Jesus Christ and, through Christ, to reveal God (John 14:7–10). This apocalyptic style was popular with Jewish and Christian writers in the centuries before and after Christ. Apocalyptic literature is known for symbolism and imagery in portraying cataclysmic events and epic battles between good and evil.

These three literature types—letter, prophesy, and apocalyptic—form a carefully composed artistic creation. In some ways, Revelation may be compared to an epic poem or complex composition of classical music. It does not proceed with all events occurring in chronological order. It sometimes resembles a collage. The book is a carefully fashioned drama, a dramatic presentation of an age-old battle between good and evil, truth and falsehood, and God and Satan. Because of Revelation's consistent use of symbolism, when in doubt, a symbolic interpretation is likely a much better choice than a literal one.

Biblical scholars agree Revelation was written in the first-century AD when Christians suffered persecution for their refusal to worship the Roman emperor. During this time, two emperors were well known for having persecuted Christians: Nero (54–68) and Domitian (81–96). Severe persecution came under Nero as a result of the great fire of Rome in AD 64. He blamed Christians and arrested, tortured, and executed hundreds. No evidence existed that they were a cause of the fire. Nero committed suicide in AD 68. Then internal chaos threatened the empire as three weak emperors reigned between June 68 and December 69.

Earlier in AD 66, Jewish zealots' opposition to Roman rule led to the Jewish/Roman War. Roman armies destroyed Jerusalem four years later. This supports a date for Revelation sometime after Jerusalem's fall in AD 70. (The earlier conquest of Jerusalem by Babylon in 587 BC is likely the reason Revelation identifies Rome as Babylon.) The attention to the New Jerusalem indicates old Jerusalem was destroyed before Revelation was written, suggesting a date after AD

70. It seems no compelling reason exists to date the book as late as the reign of Domitian. The widespread persecution under Domitian appears to have been no more severe than under Nero. Conditions within the church and the empire, supported by clues within the book, may reasonably date Revelation, in the mid to late 70s, during the reign of the emperor Vespasian.[1]

The author identifies himself as John, a popular name. Early church tradition assigns authorship of Revelation and John's gospel to the apostle John. There are significant differences between the two, but enough similarities exist to suggest a common author. Both rely heavily on symbolism and the number seven. The gospel includes seven signs (miraculous wonders) of Jesus (John 2:1–11, 4:46–54, 5:1–15, 6:5–14, 6:16–21, 9:1–7, 11:1–45) and seven "I AM" sayings of Jesus (John 5:35, 8:12, 10:7, 10:11, 11:25, 14:6, 15:5). Bearing witness and giving testimony to the truth are common themes. Only Revelation and John refer to Jesus as the Lamb and mention Jesus being pierced. Both give major attention to the Holy Spirit. Many scholars date John's gospel to about AD 85–90. If Revelation is dated AD 75–79, this allows time for both to have been written by the same author, traditionally the apostle John.[2]

Revelation divides naturally into three main sections (1:1–3:22, 4:1–19:6, 19:7–22:21), according to three titles given Jesus in 1:5: the faithful witness, the firstborn from the dead, and the ruler of kings on earth. Three detailed descriptions of Jesus's appearance (1:13–16, 5:6, 19:11–16) follow these three titles. Revelation further divides into seven sections, subdivided into seven parts. This forms a seven-act drama, each with seven scenes and a stage setting for each act.[3]

The first act is set among seven candlesticks. God's throne room in heaven sets the stage for the acts to follow. The heavenly stage settings determine the book's basic structure and transition the drama from one act to the next.

John writes to Christians living in cities where art, architecture, and literature conveyed the power and splendor of Rome and its pagan religions. Rome enjoyed peace, prosperity, and security, making its culture and religions attractive and holding the allegiance of its citizens.[4] But the velvet glove of Roman peace, the Pax Romana, covers an iron fist. The Roman state demands absolute loyalty to its imperial cult of emperor worship. Revelation creates an alternative view of Roman power and prosperity. Rome is pictured as a beast and a harlot. The churches face the dangers of pagan beliefs taking root within and graver danger coming from without, the demand on the threat of death to worship the emperor.

Revelation offers a sharp contrast to the book of Romans written by the apostle Paul. Writing this letter to Christians in Rome about AD 57, Paul tells them, "Let every person be subject to the governing authorities; for there is no authority except from God, and those authorities that exist have been instituted by God. Therefore, whoever resists authority resists what God has appointed, and those who resist will incur judgment. For rulers are not a terror to good conduct but to bad" (Romans 13:1-3).

But in Revelation, the authorities are a terror to the good conduct of those who worship the true God. Believers must resist the authorities' demands to worship the emperor. This contrast is most pronounced between Romans 13 and Revelation 13. What changed between AD 57 and AD 77? Nero!

When Paul wrote Romans, Claudius was emperor. After Nero, Roman authorities appear in a different light. Revelation is written to suffering believers who plead for justice, and John must do more than comfort and encourage his churches. He issues dire warnings of compromise and surrender to pagan religions. He meets these threats with a compelling vision to persuade and empower the churches to remain faithful in worship. In place of an iron-fisted Roman peace,

John pictures a true biblical peace (shalom), but no otherworldly peace. It is peace established through God's kingdom coming to earth. The heart of this vision of shalom is God's incomparable glory and God's great incomprehensible love revealed through the Lamb. This is the amazing love that conquered death when Jesus was bodily raised from the dead.

Using symbols and visual imagery, John urges his readers to imagine a new world with a future determined by God, not Rome. He challenges Rome with a faith-based resistance movement to affirm God and the Lamb are alone worthy of worship. This is no passive surrender to death, but resistance to evil by faithful witnesses even if at the cost of their own lives. Martyr, the Greek word for witness, came to mean someone put to death for a testimony to their faith. Jesus, the ever-faithful witness, lays down his life, staying true to his heavenly Father. The slain and standing Lamb won love's victory over sin, death, and Satan. In like manner, his followers, even in death, overcome by the blood of the Lamb.

The purpose of Revelation is to enable and empower the Church's resistance and to persuade believers to hold fast to their faith in the face of death and reject the lies of the Roman state. John insists that a fledgling Christianity must do more than passively hold fast to its faith. Believers are warned they must not exchange God's truth for the devil's lies and are challenged to fully embrace love's power. They dare not keep silent. They must be motivated to resist with their entire being and to intentionally and boldly bear witness that Jesus Christ is Lord! This is true resistance![5] The churches are thus armed with the truth of the word of God and the testimony of Jesus Christ! They are armed for worship and daily living through faith, hope, and love (1 Corinthians 13:13).

PROLOGUE (1:1–8)

The revelation of Jesus Christ, which God gave him to show his bond-servants what soon must happen; he made it known by sending his angel to his servant, John, who testified to all he saw, to the word of God and the testimony of Jesus Christ.

Blessed is the one who reads and those who hear the words of the prophecy, and who heed what is written in it. The time is near.

John, to the seven churches in Asia. Grace and peace to you from the one who is, who was, and who is coming, and from the seven spirits before his throne, and from Jesus Christ, the faithful witness, the first-born from the dead, and the ruler of the kings of the earth.

To the one who loves us and freed us from our sins by his blood, and made us a kingdom and priests to God, his Father—to him be the glory and power forever and ever. Amen.

> Look, he is coming with the clouds;
> every eye will see him,
> even those who pierced him;
> and all the earth's peoples will mourn for him.
> Amen.

The Lord God says, "I am the Alpha and the Omega, who is and who was and who is coming, the Almighty."

1–2

The revelation of Jesus Christ comes from God, who gives it to Jesus, who gives it to his angel, who gives it to John. This sequence is examined later. Angels, literally messengers, appear throughout the Bible and play a major role throughout revelation. John testifies to the word of God and testimony of Jesus Christ. In the Old Testament, two witnesses were needed to confirm the truth (Deuteronomy 19:15).

These first Christians were Jewish and knew their scriptures, the word of God (the Old Testament). They read and reread the scriptures after Jesus's death and resurrection and found that the word of God bore witness to Jesus (Acts 2). The two witnesses are the Old Testament scriptures and the apostles' oral testimony to Jesus Christ (1 John 1:1–4). The apostles and others bore witness at a great cost. Some became martyrs, dying for the truth of the word of God and the testimony to Jesus.

The apostles' oral testimony predates the written testimony later recorded in the New Testament. When John wrote Revelation, besides the Old Testament scriptures, the church already had many letters of Paul and perhaps the gospel of Mark, likely the only gospel written before AD 70. John's is more likely the last gospel written, probably about AD 85. Both John and Revelation rely on two witnesses to confirm the truth.

The Father testifies to the Son, the Son testifies to himself, and their testimony is true (John 8:17–18). Jesus says two witnesses testify about him: The Holy Spirit and the testimony of the apostles who were with him from the beginning of his ministry (John 15:26–27). The Holy Spirit is the Spirit of truth (John 14:17, 15:26). Revelation portrays a battle between good and evil, God and Satan, and truth and falsehood. Witness and truth are vital to Revelation's message.

3

Blessed are those who read, hear, and heed the words of the prophecy. Jesus often refers to those who have ears to hear. To hear is to heed and to do! The Greek language of the New Testament uses two words for time: *Chronos* (time measured in hours, days, months, and years) and *Kairos* (time as an opportunity seeking a response). For example, 6:00 a.m. is Chronos time, but if it's time to get up for work, it's also Kairos time. Kairos is the time to heed and respond. It's time to be ready and act promptly. Suffering is coming, and the churches must be ready with the word of God and testimony of Jesus Christ.

4

John writes to seven churches in Asia Minor (modern-day Turkey). "Grace and peace," a traditional Christian greeting, comes from God, Jesus, and the Holy Spirit and expresses a divine equality. First, the message comes from God, who is, who was, and who is to come. Read Exodus 3:1–14 to see why John speaks of God in this way. Moses, while shepherding the sheep of his father-in-law, approaches a bush that is burning with fire, yet not burned up. God gives Moses a mission to lead his people out of slavery in Egypt. God reveals the divine name. In Hebrew, it's YHWH. Hebrew was written then with only consonants; context determined vowels. Although once thought to be Jehovah, recent Bible scholars identify the divine name as Yahweh. *Y* and *J* sound similar in Hebrew, as do *W* and *V*. Yahweh is derived from *Hayah*, the verb "to be." God's name is I AM. God is the Great I AM who is, who was, and who is to come.

John identifies the Holy Spirit, the third member of an early expression of the Holy Trinity, as the Seven Spirits (4:5). The number seven stands for perfection, completion, and wholeness (see introduction). The number seven expresses the fullness of the Holy Spirit (Zechariah 4:6; Isaiah 11:1–2). The Holy Spirit (the Seven

Spirits) is identified with God as seven lamps before the throne (4:5) and with Jesus as seven eyes sent into all the earth (5:6). The Holy Spirit is fully and wholly equal to God and Jesus.

5–6

Jesus Christ is the faithful witness. John's vision of the exalted Christ is expanded later (9–20). Jesus is faithful to death on the cross; his followers are likewise urged to be faithful to death. He is faithful and true (19:11). Christ is faithful and true to his Father and the Spirit. He is faithful to himself and his mission. He is indeed the faithful (and true) witness. Our word *martyr*, from the Greek word for *witness*, came to mean "the one faithful to death." The firstborn of the dead is a description of Jesus expanded later in John's vision of the Lamb standing as if slain (5:6). Jesus is risen from the grave, unlike the firstborn of Egypt, who die in the final plague (Exodus 11:5) unprotected by the Passover Lamb's blood (Exodus 12).

Jesus, the Passover Lamb of the new Exodus, rescues his people by his own blood. In scripture, blood represents the life force. The blood of Jesus represents his life poured out to achieve God's victory over the powers of death and darkness (Colossians 1:13–14).

Jesus is the firstborn of the dead (his resurrection), the first of those who are to be raised later (1 Corinthians 15:20–28). He is the ruler over all earthy kings, the King of Kings and Lord of Lords (19:11–16; and introduction). Jesus now reigns in heaven at God's right hand, where all authority in heaven and on earth has been given to him (Matthew 28:18). Jesus is the faithful witness who loves us. He is the firstborn of the dead who released us from our sins by his blood. He is the ruler of the kings of the earth who has made us to be a kingdom of priests to his God and Father (Colossians 1:13–20).

In love, Jesus shed his blood for the forgiveness of our sins (1 Corinthians 15:3). He loves us. Oh yes, how he loves us. It's all by grace and how he loves us. He made us to be a kingdom of priests (Exodus 19:6; 1 Peter 2:9–10) to his God and Father (Mark 14:36). For his is the kingdom, the power, and the glory! Thank you, Lord Jesus!

7

Jesus is coming with the clouds (Daniel 7:13–14). In Daniel, the Son of Man is coming with the clouds of heaven to the Ancient of Days (Almighty God). He is coming in heaven to receive his everlasting kingdom and to reign over the earth. Throughout the gospels, Jesus self-identifies as the Son of Man. After his resurrection, at his ascension, he comes to his Father with the clouds of heaven (Acts 1:9–11) to receive his kingdom. He is Lord over all heaven and earth (Philippians 2:9–11). All who pierced him see him (Zechariah 12:10; John 19:31–34). In some way, we have all pierced him with our sin, and every eye will see him (20:12).

8

The Lord God is the Alpha and the Omega, the first and last letters in the Greek alphabet. The Lord God is the beginning and end of all things (Isaiah 41:4, 44:6, 48:12). This is one of only two times God speaks directly in Revelation. God uses this self-declaration each time; the other is in 21:5–8.

Christ also uses the same phrase twice (1:17, 22:13). Both use the expression as a sign of equality between Father and Son. The Lord God is who is, who was, and who is to come (1:4). The Almighty is another divine name (Genesis 17:1; Numbers 24:4). God is all-powerful, the supreme authority. God is supreme in love and power. He is supreme in his grace, which we need every hour.

The prologue in a Greek drama acted as an introduction. The three supreme actors of this great drama have made their introductions: The Father, the Son, and the Holy Spirit. Revelation gives an early view of the Son and Spirit in equality with God. Later the church expressed this mystery of divine equality with the doctrine of the Holy Trinity. The time has come to lift the curtain and see the stage setting, as act 1 of the drama begins.

ACT I

Stage Setting (1:9–20)

Christ among the Candlesticks

I, John, your brother, and companion, share with you in Jesus, the suffering, the kingdom, and perseverance. I was on the island Patmos because of the word of God and the testimony of Jesus Christ. I was in the Spirit on the Lord's day, and I heard behind me a loud voice like a trumpet, saying, "Write what you see in a scroll, and send it to the seven churches: to Ephesus and Smyrna and Pergamum and Thyatira and Sardis and Philadelphia and Laodicea."

Then I turned to see the voice speaking to me. And having turned, I saw seven golden lampstands; and among the lampstands, I saw someone like a son of man, wearing a robe reaching to his feet, with a golden sash wrapped across his chest. The hairs of his head were white as wool, white as snow; his eyes were like flames of fire. His feet were like bronze glowing in a furnace, and his voice sounded like rushing waters. He held seven stars in his right hand, and a sharp, two-edged sword came out of his mouth. His face shone like the sun at midday.

When I saw him, I fell, like a dead man, at his feet. But he placed his right hand on me, saying, "Do not be afraid, I am the first and the last, and the living one. I was dead; and look, I am alive forevermore and I have the keys of Death and Hades. Write, therefore, what you have seen, what is, and what is to take place after this. And this is the mystery of the seven stars, which you saw in my right hand, and the seven golden lampstands: The seven stars are the angels of the seven churches, and the seven lampstands are the seven churches."

9–10

The stage curtain rises on Act I of this great Revelation drama. John is on Patmos, a small, rocky, twelve-square mile island in the Aegean Sea off the coast of Asia Minor (modern-day Turkey). With fellow believers in Jesus, he shares their suffering, their hope in the kingdom of God, and their steadfast endurance in this time of trial. Being in the Spirit is a visionary experience (4:2, 17:3, 21:10). It's the Lord's day, resurrection day, the first day of the week.

11–12

A trumpet-sounding voice commands, "Write what you see and send it to the seven churches." Seven represents completion and a union of heaven (the Trinity) and earth (the four directions). Seven churches stand for all churches. John hears, turns around, and sees seven golden lampstands. The context is the seven-branched lampstand in the tabernacle (Exodus 25:31–37, 40). In the biblical tradition, God dwells on earth among the worshiping community, first in the wilderness tabernacle and later in the Jerusalem temple. These earthly temples represent God's dwelling place in a sacred space where heaven and earth are joined. The heavenly scenes in Revelation are pictured with earthly furnishings as shadows of the heavenly ones (Hebrews 8:5).

13

A curtain (veil) in the tabernacle and temple divided the sacred space into two rooms: the outer room (Holy Place) and innermost room (Holy of Holies). Only the priests entered the Holy Place; only the high priest entered the Holy of Holies (Hebrews 9:1–7). As John turns, he is amazed to see one like a Son of Man. He wears the robe of the high priest as he walks among the lampstands. It's Jesus, our High Priest and faithful witness, present among the churches (Hebrews 2:17). By his death, Jesus rips away the veil between the Holy Place and Holy of Holies (Mark 15:37–38). He gives direct access to the throne of God (Hebrews 10:19–25), conveyed in symbolism as he walks among the lampstands (churches) bringing believers into the Holy Place. This act prepares his people to be priests of God (verse 6). Jesus identifies himself as the Son of Man (Matthew 8:20, 9:6, etc.). This may express his humanity, but the heavenly Son of Man (Daniel 7:13–14) emphasizes his divinity.

14–16

Christ's awesome presence reflects the glory of God (John 1:14) and his own kingly rule. The exalted Christ shares the wisdom of God as shown by his white hair (Daniel 7:9). Eyes, like flames of fire, reveal his penetrating insight. His feet, like glowing bronze, give a sure foundation (Ezekiel 1:7). His voice, like rushing waters (Ezekiel 1:24), is like God's voice (Isaiah 43:2; Revelation 14:2, 19:6). The two-edged sword will be discussed later (19:15). His face shines brighter than the sun at noonday (21:23). He is the Light of the world (John 8:12), the light no darkness can overcome (John 1:5). Jesus, may your Light keep on shining in us, your people! Shine, Jesus, shine! Ever shine in us.

17–18

John falls prostrate in fear (in awe) and worship before the exalted Christ. Do not be afraid! These are familiar words of Jesus (Matthew 28:10; Luke 5:10; John 6:20). As the First and the Last (1:8), Jesus pronounces himself one with the Father. He is the Living One, raised from the grave, and holds the keys to death and Hades. This is the Greek form of the Hebrew, Sheol. Like Hades, Sheol was understood as an underworld or realm of the dead (Genesis 37:35; Job 7:9; Psalm 49:15; Proverbs 15:11; Isaiah 38:10; Ezekiel 32:27; Habakkuk 2:5).

19-20

John is instructed to write what he has seen, what is, and what is to take place after this. No chronological progression of visions or events can be assumed. The worldview of first-century Jews and Christians should be considered. They divided time into two ages: this age and the age to come (Mark 10:29–30; Luke 20:34–35). The position taken here is this: *What is* refers to what happens in the present age. *What is to take place after this* refers to the age to come. What he has *seen* refers to all John's visions. His visions are often clothed in the symbolism of the expected last days of this age, a day of reckoning (Isaiah 2:12; Joel 3:14).

The angels are God's messengers. The stage is set with Christ walking among the candlesticks. Christ walks among the churches (Matthew 28:20). The seven candlesticks also represent today's church. Jesus still walks among us, where two or three are gathered in his name (Matthew 18:20). The scenes will unfold, revealing Jesus's words of praise or rebuke. Come, Lord Jesus! Please walk among us. Though we are unworthy, may your grace embrace us, and may your rebuke turn us around. Mercifully walk among us, Jesus, that we also may walk in your grace!

ACT I

The Seven Churches (2:1–3:22)

The Church of First Love Let Go (2:1–7)

To the angel of the church in Ephesus write: "The words of the one who holds the seven stars in his right hand, who walks among the seven golden lampstands.

"I know your deeds and your labor and perseverance, that you cannot tolerate those who are evil, and you tested those who claim to be apostles, who are not; you found them to be false. You have persevered and endured for my name's sake and have not grown weary. But I hold this against you that you have let go your first love. Remember how far you have fallen, and repent. Do the deeds you did at first. Unless you repent, I am coming to you and will remove your lampstand from its place. But this you have, that you hate what I hate, the deeds of the Nicolaitans.

"Whoever has an ear, hear the Spirit's message for the churches. The one who overcomes, I will give the right to eat of the tree of life in the paradise of God."

1

Each scene of act I is a letter addressed to one of seven churches,[6, 7] known personally by John, a message to be read aloud as the people gathered for worship. Ephesus, the most important city in the region, had a population of over 250,000. It was known for its Temple of Artemis. With its beauty and extravagance, it was considered one of Seven Wonders of the Ancient World.

Christianity arrived through Paul and his coworkers (Acts 18:18–22, 19:1–41, 20:17–38). The pagan temples included those dedicated to the imperial cult of emperor worship. The church is praiseworthy for its good deeds, hard work, and perseverance and has endured for Christ's namesake. In their favor, they seem to be resisting false teachers (false apostles). Paul had warned the Ephesian elders of savage wolves coming in among the flock (Acts 20:29).

2–6

Yet good deeds and hard work are not enough because they let go of their first love. The church in Ephesus is warned of letting go of their first love for Jesus, letting go of the only love that matters. John makes a comparison to the nation of Israel, which had let go of their first love for the true God to go after idols (Jeremiah 2:2). This is a church desperately needing repentance. Not just expressing regret or feeling sorry, repentance is literally to turn around. To do the right thing, the church must return to deeds done at first, their first love for Christ and one another. If love is let go, all is lost (1 Corinthians 13). They are commended for hating the deeds of the Nicolaitans.

7

Jesus speaks to the church through the Spirit. Turn around! It's not too late! Who has ears to hear? Those who recover their first love and persevere and keep on keeping on, to hold tightly the word of

God and the testimony of Jesus Christ. Those who overcome who are victorious over the dark deadly forces within and without the church will eat of the Tree of Life (Genesis 2:9; Revelation 22:2). The Artemis Temple had a fabulous garden with a special tree as a sacred shrine, far inferior to the Tree of Life in the Paradise of God, the garden of Eden (Genesis 2:9). The Tree of Life and the lampstands are both symbols for light and life in God's presence. Those who overcome will know the true joy only God can give!

The Poor Little Rich Church (2:8–11)

And to the angel of the church in Smyrna write: "The words of the first and the last, who was dead and lives.

"I know your suffering and your poverty (yet you are rich) and the blasphemy of those who say they are Jews but are not; they are a synagogue of Satan. Do not fear what you are about to suffer. Look, the devil is about to throw some of you in prison to test you, and you will suffer persecution for ten days. But be faithful even to death and I will give you the crown of life.

Whoever has an ear, hear the Spirit's message for the churches. The one who overcomes will not be harmed by the second death."

8

A new scene begins with the reading of Christ's message to the church at Smyrna. This city of 200,000 was known for its many beautiful buildings and as the birthplace of Homer, the epic poet. (Smyrna is the only one of the seven cities still an active city today; it's now known as Izmir in modern-day Turkey.) The city enjoyed a lasting relationship with Rome, having taken Rome's side at a crucial time during its long struggle against the Carthaginian Empire (265–146 BC).

With these strong ties to Rome, the cult of emperor worship thrived in Smyrna. The cult became a growing threat to Christianity. The elderly bishop, Polycarp, a famous martyr of the early church, was put to death here in AD 155.

9–10

The church at Smyrna, this poor little rich church, seemed poor but had the true riches (2 Corinthians 8:9). Blessed are you, poor little rich church (Luke 6:20). These earliest Christians were Jewish. They believed Jesus fulfilled Judaism's promises and prophecies (Acts 2). They considered themselves the true Jews. Having found in Jesus this priceless pearl of faith (Matthew 13:44–46), they wanted all the Jewish people to share in their treasure. But it was not to be. Conflict arose between Jewish Christians and those Jews who had rejected faith in Jesus.

The apostle Paul is an early example of the conflict between Jews and Jewish Christians. Paul, a strict Jew before finding faith in Christ, had been a brutal foe of the early Christians (Acts 8:3). Immediately after his conversion to Christ, he changed into a dynamic witness for the faith he had once tried to destroy (Acts 9; Galatians 1:13). The devil gets the blame as Jews persecuted Christians; and the Jewish community was labeled a synagogue of Satan. (These unfortunate verses have been used to promote anti-Semitism throughout church history.)

Jews fight Christians, Christians fight Jews, and the devil sticks to his role of fighting against God. But the devil is a certain loser in an age-old conflict between good and evil. All numbers in Revelation are symbolic. Ten indicates a round number, a short period of time, a limited time of persecution at the hands of the Roman authorities.

11

Jesus, speaking through the Spirit, asks, "Who has ears to hear?" Those with the true riches of faith. Those who overcome, remain faithful to Jesus at the cost of their lives, are not overcome by a fear of death, and receive the crown of life. There's no more death! Only abundant life (John 10:10)!

The Church in Satan's Neighborhood (2:12–17)

To the angel of the church in Pergamum write: "The words of the one with the sharp two-edged sword.

"I know where you live, where Satan's throne is; yet you hold firm to my name and did not deny my faith; even in the days of Antipas, my faithful witness, who was killed among you, where Satan lives. But I have some things against you, because you have some who hold the teaching of Balaam, who taught Balak to throw a stumbling block before the people of Israel, to eat food sacrificed to idols and commit immorality. And you have some also who hold the teaching of the Nicolaitans. Therefore repent; else I am coming to you quickly, and war against then with the sword of my mouth.

"Whoever has an ear, hear the Spirit's message for the churches. The one who overcomes, I will give some of the hidden manna; and I will also give a white stone with a new name written on it, known only to the one who receives it."

12

Act 1 continues with the reading of Christ's message to the church at Pergamum. The name in Greek means "citadel," a fitting name for a city built on a hill a thousand feet above the river valley below. Pergamum was the capital city of the region, with many spectacular buildings made of black stone with names attached in contrasting white marble. It was the seat of the Roman governor for an entire region. The Roman authorities freely pronounce the death penalty (bear the sword) if Christians refuse to worship the emperor. But Christ bears the two-edged sword of the Word of God, a reminder of the higher power.

13-16

In a study in contrast, Satan's throne opposes God's throne. The church lives in Satan's neighborhood, where Satan dwells. Believers face dangers everywhere, pagan religions, and Rome. Of these seven cities, the dangers of being a Christian are greatest in Pergamum, with its impressive altar of Zeus, a gathering place for four major pagan cults. Antipas was martyred here for refusing to honor the imperial cult. Antipas, like his Lord, was a faithful witness.

The church faces danger from false teachings of those who are eating food sacrificed to idols and practicing fornication, a reference to Balaam (Numbers 22–25:1–3, 31:8, 16) and the Nicolaitans (2:6), who appear also to be believers with a pagan background. In a city filled with pagan temples, each temple held an image of its god. Animal sacrifice was a part of any pagan ritual, and it was considered idolatry to participate in these rituals. The early church held firm against eating meat that had been sacrificed to idols, which they believed could become a step toward idol worship (1 Corinthians 8:1–13; Acts 15:19–20). The Bible compares faithfulness to God to marriage. And turning from the true God to idols is an immoral act (Acts 15:29).

17

Repentance is urgent. The time is now. Who will overcome? Those who hold on and resist the evil one, and are faithful to death. They will receive the hidden manna, just as Israelites were fed manna in the wilderness (Exodus 15:1–5). The faithful receive white stones with new names (Isaiah 62:2), which only they know. Abraham (Genesis 17:5), Jacob (Genesis 32:28), and Peter (John 1:42) are Biblical examples of receiving a new name. Jesus offers a new name, a new identity. He still speaks through the Holy Spirit. Who has ears to hear?

The Church Holding Fast for Dear Life (2:18–29)

To the angel of the church in Thyatira write: "The words of the Son of God who has eyes like flames of fire and feet like glowing bronze.

"I know your deeds, your love and faith, your service and perseverance; and your deeds now are greater than at first. But I have this against you that you tolerate the woman, Jezebel, who claims to be a prophet and leads my servants astray by her teaching, so that they commit acts of immorality and eat food sacrificed to idols. I gave her time to repent, but she does not wish to repent of her immorality. Look, I will throw her on a sick bed, and will make those who commit adultery with her suffer greatly; unless they repent of her deeds. I will kill her children with plague, and all the churches will know I am the one who searches minds and hearts; each of you will receive according to your deeds. But I say to the rest of you in Thyatira, who do not hold this teaching and have not known the deep things of Satan; I place no other burden on you. Only hold fast to what you have until I come.

"The one who overcomes, who keeps my deeds to the end,

I will give authority over the nations,
and that one shall shepherd them with an iron rod; as
when vessels of pottery are broken,

as also I have received authority from my Father. I will give him the morning star. Whoever has an ear, hear the Spirit's message for the churches."

18

In another scene, it's another message. Thyatira, a prosperous city in the fertile Lycus river valley, is the smallest of the seven cities, less than 30,000. It's on major trade routes and known for its metal works in copper and bronze. It's home to Lydia, a seller of purple fabrics (Act 16:14–15). A wide variety of trades flourished here: leather workers, dyers, garment makers, tailors, cobblers, weavers, potters, metal workers, blacksmiths, stone cutters, and so forth. Joining trade guilds was a major part of economic life for tradespeople. This was where Christians were continually confronted by pagan religious cults. Local coins celebrated Tyrimnos, the patron deity of the bronze trade. The emperor, who was called "son of god," appears on coins in Thyatira. This showed an obvious contrast to Jesus, the true Son of God.

19–25

This is a church holding fast for dear life. At first it doesn't look that way. The church in Thyatira is known for its praiseworthy deeds of love, service, and perseverance in the faith. Their last deeds are even more commendable than the first. But Jesus, whose feet are like glowing bronze (which mirrors the local bronze metal), knows this church lacks a sure foundation. With his keen piercing eyes, glowing like fire, he sees the truth. Although their deeds are good, the bad destroyed the good. This must be addressed at once. The church is tolerating a Jezebel-like woman in their midst.

This is yet another example of the pagan practices, the deep things of Satan that have crept into the churches. Jezebel, one of the Bible's most despicable persons, worshiped idols and destroyed her neighbor.

She violated the two fundamental commandments: the love of God and the love for neighbor (1 Kings 21; 2 Kings 9). Jezebel met a bitter end, and the church is traveling in that same direction. This Jezebel-like woman has been given time to repent, and yet she has no interest in doing so. She must be cast out now! Good and evil are in constant conflict. The good must prevail. Vigilance is a must!

26–29

Verse 27 quotes from Psalm 2:9 (12:5, 19:15). It may also be roughly translated, "He shall shepherd them with a shepherd's club." The rod was a shepherd's club. Good rulers were thought of as shepherds who looked after the people. Some, like David, had been real shepherds. The shepherd carried a staff and rod (Psalm 23). The staff was a long stick with a crook to guide or catch the sheep. The rod was a stout wooden club with iron attached to one end. It protected the sheep and shepherd from wild animals and robbers.

The rod is Jesus's symbol of authority to protect his flock. The morning star (22:16) was usually Venus, brightest of the planets. As the Light of the world, Jesus shines brighter. He always shines in the darkness to light our way (John 1:5). Jesus speaks through the Spirit. Those who hold fast to him for dear life will overcome. Hold on a little longer. Don't let go! Who has ears to hear?

The Church on Life Support (3:1–6)

To the angel of the church in Sardis write: "He who has the seven Spirits of God and the seven stars, says.

"I know your deeds; you have a name for being alive, but you are dead. Wake up; strengthen what things remains. I have not found your deeds fulfilled in my God's sight. Remember what you have received and heard; hold it fast and repent. If you do not wake up, I will come like a thief and you will not know what hour I will come.

Yet you have a few people in Sardis who have not soiled their clothes. They are worthy and will walk with me in white.

The one who overcomes will be clothed in white garments; I will not erase his name from the book of life and I will confess his name before my Father and his angels. Whoever who has an ear, hear the Spirit's message for the churches."

1

In a new scene, Christ's message is read aloud in the church at Sardis. This city built on a steep hill foolishly felt safe and secure from invasion, but in 546 BC, the Persian army attacked in the night and conquered the city. Before the city residents awoke, it was too late. No wonder John's urgent warning. A thief coming at an unexpected hour is a frequent warning in scripture (16:15, 1 Thessalonians 5:2; Matthew 24:42–43). This wealthy city was favorably located on important east-west trade routes. Textile manufacturing, jewelry trade, and dye industry brought much wealth to the city through commercial trade.

2–4

Along with the church's great wealth came great wickedness. The city was known for its pagan temples with their idol worship and moral depravity. This church's reputation may have been good, but what God sees is not worthy of being commended. This church in grave danger must soon wake up. It's more dead than alive, a church on life support. But due to grace, the plug has not yet been pulled. How many righteous believers will it take to save this church (Genesis 18:22–33)? Are there enough who have kept their clothes unsoiled? There are lots of clean clothes readily available in a city known for its textile manufacturing.

5–6

A much greater need exists for moral cleanliness. More believers are needed, those who wear white robes for purity and victory. More are needed who are worthy to wear white (Ecclesiastes 9:8). More are desperately needed who have overcome life's struggle against evil. This church, more dead than alive, is a church on life support needing the Seven Spirits (the Holy Spirit).

Come, Holy Spirit, come. Come from the four winds; blow the breath of life. Breathe your life where death has the upper hand. Breathe, Spirit. Keep on blowing and breathe your new life (Ezekiel 37). Breathe that this church, as good as dead, may stand up for Jesus. Breathe, Spirit, that it may stand up and live and heed the Lord's words. May all those having ears to hear soon hear. May they soon confess the name of Jesus. Are there yet ears to hear the Spirit's message?

The Church of the Open Door (3:7–13)

To the angel of the church in Philadelphia write:

> "The words of the one who is holy and true
>   who has the key of David,
>   who opens and no one shuts,
>   who shuts and no one opens.

"I know your deeds; look, I have put before you an open door that no one can shut; because you have little power, and have kept my word and have not denied my name. Look, I will cause those of the synagogue of Satan, who say they are Jews, and are not, but are lying, to come bow at your feet and acknowledge I have loved you. Because you have kept my word and persevered, I will keep you from the hour of testing, an hour to come upon the whole world, to test those who live on earth. I am coming quickly; hold fast to what you have, so no one will take your crown.

"The one who overcomes, I will make him a pillar in the temple of my God; he will never leave it. And I will write on him the name of the city of my God, the new Jerusalem, which comes down out of heaven from my God, and my new name. Whoever has an ear, hear the Spirit's message to the churches."

7

Philadelphia was called the gateway to the East. A powerful earthquake had destroyed most of the city less than fifty years earlier. A major road from Rome to Troas ran through the city, located on a fertile plain where many grapes grew. Jesus is the one who is holy and true. (The contrast between truth and lie appears throughout Revelation.) Like the royal steward (Isaiah 22:22), Jesus has the key of David. With this key, the church has an open door, a door that no one can shut. A church with little power of their own is a church with the true power of God's word and love.

8–11

There is no hiding of God's love behind closed doors. God gives an open door for proclaiming the gospel. With a wide-open door, this little church knows the true joy of sharing Jesus's love. Their deeds are well known, meaning their love for one another in the city of brotherly love.

A well-established Jewish community of thousands lived in Philadelphia in contrast to a small band of Christians, who were often badly outnumbered by Jews in cities of Asia. (Scripture has been used as justification for centuries of anti-Semitism and cruel persecution of the Jews.) Persecution by Rome was expected soon. As a church known for its perseverance, these believers must hold fast to their faith, as future suffering comes to the churches and emperor worship is demanded of all.

12–13

Once an earthquake brought magnificent temples and their great pillars crashing down. Pillars are foundation material; Philadelphia is a foundation church. The one who overcomes will be a pillar in God's temple in times of trial. This is the first reference in Revelation to the New Jerusalem. The city of Jerusalem had been recently destroyed when this letter was written. The loss of the old Jerusalem gives the context for the promised New Jerusalem.

Jesus is the new temple (John 2:18–21). Therefore, his body, the church, is God's temple, the Holy Spirit's residing place. This church of the open door is sharing Christ's love, not living by power or might, but living by the Spirit (Zachariah 4:6). God makes all things new! Whoever has an ear, let them hear the Spirit speaking.

The Church about to Be Spit Out (3:14–22)

To the angel of the church in Laodicea write: "The words of the Amen, the faithful and true witness, the beginning of God's creation.

"I know your deeds; you are neither cold or hot; I wish you were either cold or hot. But because you are lukewarm, neither cold or hot, I will spit you out of my mouth. because you say you are rich, have become wealthy and need nothing; yet you do not know you are wretched and miserable and poor and blind and naked. I counsel you to buy from me gold refined by fire so you may become rich, and white garments so you may clothe yourself and not reveal the shame of your nakedness, and eye salve to anoint your eyes so you may see. I reprove and discipline those I love, so be zealous and repent. Listen! I stand at the door and knock. If anyone hears my voice and opens the door, I will come in and we will dine with each other.

"The one who overcomes I will grant him to sit down with me on my throne, just as I overcame and sat down with my Father on his throne. Whoever has an ear, hear the Spirit's message to the churches."

14

Laodicea is mentioned four times in the letter to the Colossians (2:1, 4:13, 15–16). This was a wealthy city. built on major trade routes and known for its textile industry, banking, and medical school.

This city on the Lycus River had other sources for water in times of drought. Hot mineral springs, five miles north at Hierapolis, supplied lukewarm water, loaded with minerals but hardly drinkable when it reached Laodicea. The city piped water from cold mountain streams fed by snow-capped mountains near Colossae, eleven miles to the southeast, but by the time this water reached Laodicea, it was also only lukewarm.

15-20

This is a familiar, vivid image: The church at Laodicea, just like the water, was lukewarm; a church about to be spit out of Jesus's mouth. It only seems to be a wealthy church; Jesus's gifts are far superior to their bank's fleeting riches. He gives true wealth, golden deeds of love and mercy refined by the fire of suffering. White robes, for purity and victory, are contrasted with the black garments made with wool from the local black sheep. Their medical school exported a powder used for eye salve, but only Jesus can anoint their eyes for blindness, which hides the true riches.

Jesus's gracious words of invitation are, "I stand at the door and knock." There is a famous painting of Jesus knocking at the door by the English artist William Holman Hunt (1827–1910). Other artists have painted this scene as well. As a stained-glass artist, I have my own depiction of Jesus knocking at the door. Jesus desires to enter and share a meal, an act of true Christian fellowship and community.

21-22

The throne is the symbol of God's rule and authority as king over the universe. God has exalted Jesus to share his reign (Philippians 2:9–11). Believers are to share in Christ's reign on earth (5:10). Those who overcome may join Jesus at the throne of God.

With no pause that refreshes for a lukewarm church, Christ makes a last plea to overcome and heed the Spirit. Judgment looms, yet amazing grace abounds. As the curtain closes on act I, this image of Jesus lingers. He's knocking, listening intently for the sound of our footsteps, waiting for someone to open the door.

ACT II

Stage Setting (4:1–5:13)

The Heavenly Throne Room (4:1–11)

After this I looked, and saw a door standing open in heaven; and the voice, like a trumpet, which I had heard speaking to me at first, said, "Come up here, and I will show you what must take place after this." At once, I was in the Spirit, and saw a throne standing in heaven, and one sitting on the throne. The one sitting was like jasper stone and a sardius in appearance. A rainbow, looking like an emerald, encircled the throne. I saw twenty-four thrones around the throne, and twenty-four elders seated on the thrones, dressed in white, and golden crowns on their heads.

Out from the throne, lightning flashed, voices sounded and thunder rumbled. Before the throne, seven lamps were burning; these are the seven Spirits of God. And before the throne I saw what looked like a sea of glass, clear as crystal; in the center around the throne, were four living creatures, full of eyes, in front and in back. The first living creature was like a lion, the second like an ox, the third had a face like a human figure, and the fourth was like a flying eagle. And each of the four living creatures had six wings, and were full of eyes, front and back. And day and night they never cease to say,

"Holy, holy, holy
is the Lord God, the Almighty,
who was and who is and who is to come."

And as the living creatures give glory, honor and thanks to him who sits on the throne, who lives forever and ever, the twenty-four elders fall before him who sits on the throne and worship him who lives forever and ever, and cast their crowns before the throne, saying,

"Worthy are you, our Lord and our God,
to receive glory, honor, and power;
for you created all things,
and by your will they existed and were created.

1

The heavenly throne room sets the stage for act II of the grand Revelation drama. This is the sacred heart of all the visions that John has seen (1:19). As the curtain rises for act II, he sees a door open in heaven (Ezekiel 1:1) and hears a voice saying, "Come up here." It's Jesus, whose trumpet-like voice he heard earlier (1:10–11). Referring to heaven as up means a higher authority, not a direction (Isaiah 55:9). Heaven may be best explained as a dimension of reality beyond the four dimensions we know through our senses, one which eye has not seen, ear heard, or humans imagined (1 Corinthians 2:9).

God and heaven are portrayed symbolically, yet words or symbols prove insufficient to express God's unimaginable glory. When John says "after this," it may refer to the order in which he receives the visions but not necessarily a chronological sequence of events. This stage setting pictures God's sovereign reign over the world existing from all eternity (Psalm 103:19).

2–4

John is in the Spirit. The Old Testament prophets recorded similar visionary experiences (Isaiah 6:1–10; Ezekiel 1:1–28; 11:22–25). John hears the voice of Jesus. Then the Spirit enables him to see the vision (1:10, 4:2). After hearing the voice speaking to him, John sees the throne and the one sitting on the throne (Isaiah 6:1; Daniel 7:9). The throne is a well-known symbol of God's authority and rule in heaven and on earth (1 Kings 22:19; Psalm 47:8). In Isaiah 6:1, God's glory in the temple appears to fill the earth. God's presence is revealed with the brilliance of precious stones and a rainbow (Ezekiel 1:28). These stones are among those displayed on the high priest's breastplate (Exodus 28:17). They magnify and reflect the light that hides the unapproachable glory of God (Psalm 104:2). The rainbow is a reminder of the covenant with Noah and remains a universal symbol of God's mercy and grace (Genesis 9:13).

John sees twenty-four smaller thrones arranged around the center throne, with twenty-four seated elders. These heavenly beings ceaselessly serve the one sitting on the throne as models for God's people on earth: twelve tribes of the old covenant and twelve apostles of the new (Israel and church). Multiples of twelve appear frequently to represent the people of God. The elders wear crowns, expressing the royal priesthood of God's people (1:6). Their robes are white for victory and purity.

5

Special attention is given this phrase, "Out from the throne lightning flashed, voices sounded and thunder rumbled." It's an echo of God's awesome appearance on Mt. Sinai (Exodus 19:16). This transition verse reoccurs in the drama (8:5, 11:19, 16:18). In the larger context in Exodus 19:1–25, the people are warned: Get back! Don't dare get close to the mountain! God is appearing! A sinful people dare not go near a holy God. Only God's representatives, Moses, and Aaron, may draw near. If the people get too close, judgment for sin will fall upon them. Keeping a safe distance holds judgment back. Similar warnings keep coming in following acts, but each time when judgment seems certain to fall, its full force is held back. God continues to seek salvation for his wayward people. God is the God of Exodus and the God of Revelation, the God of glory and the God of grace.

The seven lamps of fire before God's throne (1:4) are the seven Spirits of God (Zechariah 4:1–6). The lamps are modeled after the seven-branched lampstand in the Holy Place of the tabernacle (Exodus 40:24–25). The lamps, which represent the seven churches (1:20), now show the Spirit's presence as a true light in every church. The Spirit acts as the go-between God by shining the glory of God into our own lives. The Spirit's grace-full light reveals our brokenness and heals our sin. Come, Holy Spirit. Come as the fire and burn with God's glory. Come as the light and shine with God's grace. Come, Holy Spirit! We need you! Come Holy Fire, we pray! Make us whole by the grace of our Lord Jesus Christ!

6–7

The amazing scene at God's throne continues with four living creatures. Creatures from an outer galaxy? No, symbols of God's creation in worship: the lion for wild animals, the ox for domestic animals, the eagle for birds, and man, for the human family. Animals, trees, and fields worship. All God's good creation worships its maker (Psalm 96, 98). These living creatures are much like the living beings in Ezekiel's vision (Ezekiel 1:10). Full of eyes, they are all-seeing. The living creatures became symbols for the four gospels: Matthew (person), Mark (lion), Luke (ox), and John (eagle). Biblical symbolism of the four living creatures originates with the cherubim on the mercy seat, the lid for the ark of the covenant. In the Holy of Holies, God's presence dwelt above the wings of the cherubim. Outstretched wings represent God's throne (Exodus 25:17–22).

8–9

Holy, holy, holy! Lord God Almighty! Revelation inspires countless resources for Christian worship over the centuries. Holy, holy, holy! Four living creatures! Their never-ceasing threefold proclamation of the unapproachable holiness of God! John recalls the seraphim of Isaiah's temple vision (Isaiah 6:1–7). The elders and living creatures join in worship, honoring God with a threefold blessing. Glory and honor to God is expressed in all Revelation's blessings. Glory refers to the divine presence. God's glory fills the tabernacle (Exodus 40:34), the whole earth (Isaiah 6:3). Honor refers to reverence and value, placing worship of God above all earthy duties (Psalm 47:7–8). And thanks! Give thanks with a grateful heart!

10–11

God receives the worship due as the only Creator, the God of Genesis who created all things. God alone and no mortal is worthy of worship. To fall upon the face is an act of worship by the twenty-four elders. Casting down their golden crowns. God is worthy and holy. Glory, all glory, belongs to God—glory of light inapproachable and glory of beauty unimaginable. All glory and honor and power belong to God. Power replaces thanks in the previous blessing, the awesome power of the creator and sustainer who spoke the worlds into being (Genesis 1; Hebrews 1). Our Lord and our God, we live to give you honor, place our lives in your hands, and cast our crowns before you. Let there be glory, honor, power, and praise to the Lord God, the Almighty (4:8).

This heavenly scene is astonishing, an image of going up into God's presence and a model for the Christian life. We look up to God. God judges us. Our sin is laid bare (Hebrews 4:12–13) so God may save us. We look up to God, saved only by grace and joining in worship with God's people and sharing with all creation in the worship of the Creator. We join in celebration, looking up and rejoicing in God's creative power and wondrous deeds (Isaiah 55). We look to God's amazing grace, cling to the Lamb's wondrous love, and receive God's life-changing breath, the Holy Spirit.

The seven-branched lampstand lit the Holy Place. The holy fire of the Holy Spirit lights the way for God's people in worship and service. Spirit of God, fall fresh upon us. Cleanse us and renew us. Our Creator and Redeemer, our Lord, and our God, we were created so we may worship you! We bow before you; we worship and adore you. We cast our crowns before you! Holy! Holy! Holy! You alone are holy!

The Lamb Alone Is Worthy (5:1–14)

I saw in the right hand of the One who sat on the throne a scroll with writing on both sides and sealed with seven seals. And I saw a mighty angel proclaiming with a loud voice, "Who is worthy to open the scroll and to break its seals? But no one in heaven or on the earth or under the earth was able to open the book or to see inside it. Then I began to weep greatly because no one was found worthy to open the scroll or to see inside it. And one of the elders said to me, stop crying; look! The Lion of the tribe Judah, the root of David, has overcome. He can open the scroll and its seven seals.

Then I saw a Lamb standing, as though slain, among the throne and the four living creatures and the elders. It had seven horns and seven eyes, which are the seven Spirits of God, sent out into all the earth. And he came and took the scroll from the right hand of the One who sat on the throne. When the Lamb had taken the scroll, the four living creatures and the twenty-four elders fell before him, each elder holding a harp and golden bowls full of incense, which are the prayers of the saints. And they sang a news song, saying,

"Worthy are you to take the scroll
and to break its seals;
For you were slain, and with your blood you purchased for God
those from every tribe and tongue and people and nation.
You have made them to be a kingdom and priests to our God;
and they will reign upon the earth."

Then I looked, and I heard the voice of many angels around the throne and the living creatures and the elders. The angels numbering thousands upon thousands and ten thousand times ten thousand, are saying with a loud voice,

"Worthy is the Lamb who was slain
to receive power and riches and wisdom
and strength and honor and glory and blessing,"

And I heard every created thing which is in heaven and on the earth and under the earth and in the sea, and all that is in them, saying,

"To the one who sits on the throne, and to the Lamb,
be blessing and honor and glory and might
forever and ever."

And the four living creatures kept saying, "Amen." And the elders fell and worshiped.

1–2

The stage setting of God's throne room continues with John's vision of the slain Lamb. First, he sees the right hand of the one sitting on the throne. The right hand is a dominant hand for most persons; the symbol of power and authority. A place at the right hand is the position of high privilege (Mark 12:36; Acts 2:34; Hebrews 1:13). The seven churches are held in Jesus's right hand (1:16, 20). In Ezekiel 2:9–10, a hand appears with a scroll written on the front and back, but which hand is not stated. The scroll was a sheet of rolled parchment with writing on both sides and sealed with wax seals (Isaiah 29:11). Who is worthy to open it?

3–5

No one, in heaven or on earth or under the earth (in the realm of the dead), can be found to open the scroll. No one is deserving enough. No one is worthy! No one! John weeps bitterly. There is no one, and then suddenly there is one who is found worthy! It's the Lion! John is told that the Lion from the tribe of Judah, the root of David (Isaiah 11:1), is worthy. Judah was one of the twelve sons of Jacob, and in his father's final blessing, he is blessed as a lion (Genesis 49:8–10).

Both David and Jesus, according to the flesh, are descended from the tribe of Judah. The Messiah was expected to be from the tribe of Judah and to be a descendent of King David. The scroll will be unsealed. One who is worthy to open it has been found. Heaven and earth wait now with bated breath. The suspense builds! God is worthy, and Jesus is worthy. Worthy! The Lion of Judah is found worthy!

6

John looks but sees no lion; he sees a Lamb. The scene of God's throne room becomes even more amazing: A Lamb is standing (Jesus's resurrection) as though slain (his death). The Lamb standing as though slain is revealing the cross as God's ongoing victory. Christ's death and resurrection continue to deliver humankind from the domain of darkness (Colossians 1:13). The Lamb has overcome. He has conquered and won the victory as the faithful and true witness.

Not by being slain does Jesus become the witness, faithful and true. He is slain for already being the true and faithful witness (Mark

14:61–65). Jesus comes to testify to the truth (John 18:37), to bear witness to God's true and faithful love (John 3:16). He comes as the incarnation, as the embodiment of God's love (John 1:14) that those who see him may see the Father (John 14:9). Jesus stands up for the truth of God. He willingly lays down his life and takes it up again (John 10:15–18). Worthy! The Lamb alone is worthy!

Jesus fulfills the messianic hope. He is the conquering Davidic Messiah, bringing God's kingdom to earth, not by an expected warrior lion, but by the slain and risen Lamb. He has won the decisive victory over evil by his death and resurrection. The theme of a new Exodus connects the slain and risen Jesus to the Passover Lamb's saving blood. Jesus is the Lamb led to slaughter (Isaiah 53:7). Death never can hold the Lamb (Acts 2:24). Standing as though slain, He stands in the center of the throne (7:17). The Lamb stands in oneness with the one who is seated on the throne (likely meaning of 5:6).

Seven stands for completeness, for perfection. The horn is a symbol of power; seven horns reveal the Lamb as all-powerful (omnipotent). The seven eyes show the lamb as all-seeing, all-knowing (omniscient). Seven eyes, like the seven lamps of fire (4:5), represent the Holy Spirit (Zechariah 4:1–6). The omnipresent Lamb sends the all-seeing Spirit into all the earth (2 Chronicles 16:9; Zechariah 4:10). The Lamb, like the one seated on the throne, is all-powerful, all-seeing, and all-knowing. To see the Lamb is to see the Father's heart (John 14:9).

7–8

The Lamb takes the scroll from God's right hand (1:1). Later an angel will receive the scroll that God gave to Jesus, and it will be passed from the angel to John (from God to Jesus, to an angel, and to John). As John receives the scroll, the twenty-four elders and the four living creatures fall in worship. Worthy! You are worthy! Compare 4:9–11 with 5:8–10. First, all worship the One seated on the throne and repeat the sequence as they worship the Lamb that was slain. The Lamb stands on equal footing with the Almighty Creator God, sitting upon the throne. The elders hold harps and bowls of incense (8:3–4).

9–10

The Lamb is worthy, slain for the truth. The new song (14:3) celebrates the worthiness of the Lamb (5:9, 12) above all in heaven, on earth, and under the earth (Sheol). The Lamb shed his blood to liberate all humanity; all the ends of the earth are to see God's salvation (Psalm 98). A new song of universal praise of the Lamb is sung by those of every tribe, tongue, people, and nation. He died for all; none are excluded. God's goal is to restore all creation (Romans 8:18–25). The Lamb is worthy, for by his faithfulness, he establishes believers as and priests to God (Exodus 19:6; 1 Peter 2:8–10). Jesus, the Davidic Messiah (the Lion), brings the kingdom of God to earth as the slain and risen Lamb. Heaven is intended as a temporary stage after death. It is not meant as the place of our ultimate destiny. After this heavenly sojourn, believers are to reign upon earth as a kingdom and priests to God.

11–14

Revelation is about worship of the Creator God of Genesis (4:1–11) and the liberating God of Exodus and the cross (5:1–14). The heavenly stage fills up beyond imagination as thousands and thousands of angels (Daniel 7:10) give a sevenfold blessing. Worship of the One who sits upon the throne leads to the worship of Jesus Christ, the slain and risen Lamb. Through worship, the church retells the ancient story of the battle between good and evil, God and Satan. Revelation tells of God's victory over the father of lies.

Tell again the story of truth's victory over falsehood. John appeals to a suffering church: Remain faithful in worship. Give all glory to God and the Lamb. Lift up God's praises, no matter the cost. Keep on telling of God's victory over sin and death. The old story is never old as we tell of love, brave and bold. This tale of a Friday, when the skies turn black, as evil and sin, death, and the devil were fighting back in a mortal battle against the love of God. The faithful witness goes to his death on the cross. It looks like all is lost and death has the last word! But another story is not to be forgotten.

> Long before that dark Friday, outside the city walls:
> Look, A frightened people, watching the waves of the sea,
> Pharaoh chariots coming swiftly, behind them they see.
> But at early dawn for this people, trapped by the sea,
> The Lord God wins the battle; the slaves are set free
> (Exodus 14:24)

The Exodus narrative is woven throughout Revelation. Exodus is a preview to the story of the Lamb (Luke 9:31).

> On that frightful Friday, when all appears lost,
> When sin's dark powers battle Jesus on the cross
> They already know they have met their match.
> Evil's fiendish forces realize they made no catch.
> And it's only Friday! Then Sunday comes!

At early dawn, there is an empty tomb (Matthew 28; Mark 16; Luke 24; John 20).

> Death would never keep its prey
> when Christ arose on Easter Day.
> As the first-born of all the dead

On that Sunday, His was the victory.

Christians are Sunday people.

Christ is risen from the grave, as all God's creation sings
All God's creatures share the joy this good news brings.
The Lamb has won the victory by his death and resurrection
The kingdom comes to earth as God redeems all His creation.

Worthy is the Lamb that was slain!

It's a sign of completion,
This seven-fold blessing.
Worthy to receive power and riches
and wisdom and might and honor
and glory and blessing!

The Lamb reigns!

His work finished, all creation before him will bow.
And His church will come together in worship now.
For the churches, seven, hard times are coming.
Revelation's Drama continues as Act II is beginning.

ACT II

The Seven Seals (6:1–8:2)

The Rider on the White Horse (6:1–2)

Then I saw the Lamb open one of the seven seals, and I heard one of the four living creatures saying in a voice like thunder, "Come." And looking, I saw, a white horse, and its rider had a bow; and was given a crown; and he went our conquering, and to conquer.

1–2

Act II, scene one begins with the stage setting of the heavenly throne room. The Lamb opens each seal and introduces a new scene. All seals must be opened before the scroll's contents are known.[8] While opening the wax seals, the Lamb does not reveal future events. He shows the meaning of present-day events then occurring already on the world stage. The vision of the four horsemen includes both what John *has seen* and symbolism for the present age, *what is.* Who is the rider on a white horse? Alexander the Great? Genghis Khan? It's sure not Jesus. He appears later, on a white horse (19:11).

This rider is Jesus's evil opposite, the spirit of conquest, going forth with a bow and wearing a ruler's crown. This sounds much like Parthia, Rome's archenemy, with its skilled archers on horseback. As a symbol of conquest, the rider fits Parthia, Rome, and other conquering nations of the times. John's symbols come from scripture. The archer's bow and quiver of arrows are the lethal weapons of the day, a well-known symbol of warfare (Psalm 46:9). Babylon conquered Jerusalem in 587 BC with an army that included wave upon wave of archers (Jeremiah 51:3, 56). Babylon's previous conquest is an obvious reason for Revelation's identification of Rome as the new Babylon.

In John's churches, Rome's empire threatens to become this same conquering force, riding roughshod over their lives. The desire for conquest continues to ride on in infamy as three more riders keep on riding after it. A fearsome foursome is let loose to terrorize the world. Three more scenes follow quickly. In contrast to the desire for conquest, Revelation knows only one true conqueror above all conquerors, Jesus the Lamb, standing as though slain. Jesus the Lamb, having conquered by his death and resurrection, has completed his conquest. Jesus alone is worthy! Jesus is King over all kings on earth!

The Rider on the Fiery Red Horse (6:3–4)

And when he opened the second seal, I heard the second living creature saying, "Come." And another, a fiery red horse, went out; and its rider was permitted to take peace from the earth, so that people should slay one another; and a great sword was given to him.

3–4

The vision of the four horsemen matches the horrific conditions of the Jewish-Roman war (AD 67–70). Within Judaism, a radical party known as the Zealots had long opposed Roman rule. As their influence grew, Jesus had warned of the terrible war he saw coming within a generation. Hear his haunting words as he wept over Jerusalem, "If you had known ... the things which make for peace! But now they have been hidden from your ears ... your enemies will throw up a barricade against you ... surround you ... level you to the ground and your children within you ..." (Luke 19:41–44). (Read Matthew 24:1–51, Mark 13:1–37, and Luke 21:1–38.) These verses warn of the tragedy that would unfold after Roman forces surrounded Jerusalem. It's not a warning of the last days.

After Jesus's resurrection, the power of the Zealots continued to increase for decades. Their hit-and-run attacks against Roman forces grew bolder. Scattered opposition became pitched battles. Then, an all-out war exploded in the mid-60s. In late AD 66, Jewish forces drove the Romans out of Jerusalem, set up their own government in the city, and briefly controlled much of their homeland. Meanwhile the Roman emperor, Nero, known for his cruelty to Jews and Christians alike, sent Roman Legions to crush the rebellion.

Jews from the countryside fled to the city as its population increased dramatically. Many thousands died during the siege that followed. Many more thousands, while attempting to escape, were crucified. When the city fell, hundreds of thousands were killed, captured, and enslaved. But Christians, who remembered Jesus's warnings a generation earlier, had fled Jerusalem while escape was possible. This insatiable desire for conquest (the rider on the white horse) leads to war (the rider on the red horse), and still two more horses and their riders will follow them, riding on in infamy.

The Rider on the Black Horse and the Rider on the Pale Horse (6:5–8)

And when he opened the third seal, I heard the third living creature saying, "Come." And I looked and saw a black horse; and the rider held a pair of scales in his hand. And I heard what sounded like a voice in the center of the four living creatures saying "A quart of wheat for a denarius, and three quarts of barley for a denarius, but do not harm the oil and the wine."

And when he opened the fourth seal, I heard the voice of the fourth living creature saying, "Come," And I looked, and saw a pale horse; and the rider's name was Death; and Hades was following him. And authority was given to them over a fourth of the earth, to kill with sword, with famine and with pestilence and by the wild beasts of the earth.

5–8

The red horse and its rider follow the white horse and its rider (scenes one and two). We now examine the next two scenes of act II together: scene three, the black horse and its rider (famine), and scene four, the pale horse and its rider (death). War follows desire for conquest. Famine, disease, and death soon follow war. A denarius represented a day's wages for the poor. Basic food staples were scarce, but other items were available for those who could afford them. Roman armies had camped around Jerusalem in AD 68–69, and early 70, they cut off the city from all outside help. Hundreds of thousands died from famine and disease during this ordeal as the Romans lay siege. Jerusalem finally fell in August AD 70.

John's source of the four horses appears to come from Zachariah 6:1–8, where four teams of horses are pulling chariots. Each team is a different color with horses that are black, red, white, and dappled. The Lamb reveals these horrid horsemen to be man's own dreadful creation. Jeremiah and Ezekiel had warned of death by sword, famine, and pestilence, before and after Jerusalem fell in 587 BC (Jeremiah 38:2, 42:17). The horses and their riders mercifully leave the stage.

The Martyrs under the Altar (6:9–11)

And when he opened the fifth seal, I saw under the altar the souls of those who had been slain because of the word of God and the testimony which they had maintained. And they cried out in a loud voice, saying, "How long, O Lord, holy and true, will you keep from judging and avenging our blood on those who dwell on the earth? And each of them was given a white robe; and they were told to rest a little longer, until the testimony of their fellow servants and their brothers and sisters who were to be killed as they had been, would also be completed.

9–11

This scene introduces the martyrs. Christians were already dying under Nero's reign (AD 54–68). Then hundreds were slaughtered on a pretense they caused the fire that destroyed two-thirds of Rome in July AD 64. History places in proximity the siege and fall of Jerusalem and the martyrs' anguished cry over Nero's persecution. Altar symbolism applies to both the bronze altar for sacrifice (Exodus 27) and the golden altar of incense (Exodus 30), combining sacrifice and prayer (8:3). Is it unchristian to cry out for vengeance? Not in Romans 12:19, as vengeance belongs to a holy and true God. His wrath is a just response to the slaughter of the innocent. "How long, O Lord" is a universal plea of martyrs through the ages. How long will you forget me?! How long this heart of sorrow? How long will my enemies defeat me? (Psalm 13:1–2)

White robes the martyrs receive. Now they just rest and believe. Babylon destroyed Jerusalem in 587 BC. Exiles in Babylon wait to rebuild the old Jerusalem. In AD 70, Rome destroyed Jerusalem. Martyrs in heaven wait for God to bring to earth the New Jerusalem. To the Old, exiles wait to return. For the New, martyrs wait to return. In Revelation's unfolding drama, a rider on a white horse leaves a trail of bloodshed and Jerusalem's destruction (act II). Jesus, another rider on a white horse, leads the martyrs to the New Jerusalem and earth's restoration (act VII). The drama moves from the old to the new. Souls in heaven wait for justice, crying out, "How long!" Until New Jerusalem comes to earth and saints sing their victory song!

Scene Six: A Coming Day of Reckoning (6:12–17)

I looked when he opened the sixth seal, and a great earthquake occurred; and the sun became black as sackcloth made of hair, and the full moon became blood red; and the stars of the sky fell to the earth, as a fig tree drops its unripe figs when shaken by a strong wind. The sky departed like a scroll when it is rolled up, and every mountain and island were moved out of their places. And the kings of the earth and the princes and the commanders and the rich and the powerful and every slave and free person hid themselves in the caves and among the rocks of the mountains; and they said to the mountains and to the rocks, "Fall on us and hide us from the presence of the one seated on the throne, and from the fury of the Lamb; because the great day of their anger has come, and who is able to stand?"

12–17

The Roman Empire extended to Egypt to the south, Spain to the west, Britain to the north, and in the east to Armenia, Babylon, and its ancient foe, the Parthian Empire. Rome, at the pinnacle of its glory, still feared invasion from Parthia (sixth trumpet and sixth bowl). Rome is a classic example of arrogance, pride, and power's corrupting influence. One day, arrogance is to be humbled when God alone will be exalted. The sixth seal's message is a universal condemnation of arrogance that seeks to replace God. Pride is associated with the name, Babylon (Genesis 11:1–9). Revelation promises a coming day of reckoning (Isaiah 2:12–22). The martyrs of scene five trust God's justice, believing evil will have no last word.

Isaiah and Revelation use hyperbolic language to stress the gravity of man's sin, pride, and vanity before a holy God. Terrifying earthquakes! Sky turned black! Heaven shaking! Stars falling! All earth-shattering events! All symbolism to express God's justice for the ones who suffer, for God's judgment coming upon evil that humans inflict upon each other. This scene will soon be revisited in acts III and V. The drama uses the symbolism of humbling the proud, a very real occurrence in this present age of kings, despots, tyrants, and strong men and wannabes, where what goes around comes around.

With this scene, Revelation uses the symbolism of the last days of this age, with its hope that sufferings will make way for the glory of the age to come (Romans 8:18), where even creation suffers the pains of childbirth (Romans 8:22), an in-between time where all the lofty and proud are humbled (Isaiah 2:12–22). The drama of Revelation also plays out in the shadow of the cross, that greatest day of reckoning, when "God was in Christ reconciling the world to himself" (2 Corinthians 5:19), when a window opens into the mystery that joins the two ages and where darkness and earthquake are symbols of God's judgment and salvation (Matthew 27:45–51).

Scene Six: Vision of the Church on Earth (7:1–8)

After this I saw four angels standing at the four corners of the earth, holding back the four winds of the earth, so that no wind would blow on the earth or on the sea or on any tree. Then I saw another angel ascending from the rising of the sun, with the seal of the living God; and he cried out with a loud voice to the four angels who were allowed to harm the earth and the sea, saying, "Do not harm the earth or the sea or the trees until we have sealed the bond-servants of our God on their foreheads."

And I heard the number of those who were sealed, one hundred forty-four thousand sealed from every tribe of the sons of Israel:

> From the tribe of Judah, twelve thousand sealed,
> from the tribe of Reuben, twelve thousand,
> from the tribe of Gad, twelve thousand, from
> the tribe of Asher, twelve thousand,

from the tribe of Naphtali, twelve thousand, from
the tribe of Manasseh, twelve thousand,
from the tribe of Simeon, twelve thousand,
from the tribe of Levi, twelve thousand,
from the tribe of Issachar, twelve thousand, from
the tribe of Zebulun, twelve thousand,
from the tribe of Joseph, twelve thousand, from the
tribe of Benjamin, twelve thousand sealed.

1–3

The sixth seal is opened, and justice is surely coming. God's wrath will be poured out. Then God calls a time-out. The scene changes. Winds of judgment are held back. Revelation, like classical music, rises toward a climax and falls again, only to repeat over and over until the final crescendo.

4–8

The figure 144,000 is a symbolic number: twelve tribes x twelve apostles = 144 (God's people, Israel, and church). And then 10^3 (three is the symbol for the Trinity) is 1,000. The figure 144,000 is a round number, meaning a large multitude. The 144,000 represents the militant church, the new Israel, sealed for salvation from the coming judgment (6:12–17). They are the Lord's army, ready for battle, prepared to overcome by the blood of the Lamb (Numbers 1). The two sources for John's imagery of sealing the believers are Exodus 13:9 and 9:4. The sealing suggests the blood of the Passover Lamb on the doorposts that protected the Israelites (Exodus 12:1–13). The 144,000 are protected by the blood of the Lamb from judgment and are sealed for martyrdom.

Scene Six: Vision of the Church in Heaven (7:9–17)

After these things I looked and saw there, a great multitude which no one could count, from every nation, and all tribes and peoples and tongues, standing before the throne and before the Lamb, clothed in white robes, with palm branches in their hands. and they cry out with a loud voice, saying,

> "Salvation to our God who sits on the throne,
> and to the Lamb."

And all the angels were standing around the throne and around the elders and the four living creatures; and they fell on their faces before the throne and worshiped God, saying,

> "Amen, blessing and glory and wisdom
> and thanksgiving and honor and power
> and might, be to our God forever and ever.
> Amen"

Then one of the elders said to me, "Who are these clothed in the white robes, and where have they come from?" I said to him, "My lord, you know." And he said to me, "These are the ones who come out of the great suffering, and they have washed their robes in the blood of the Lamb and made them white.

> "Therefore, they are before the throne of God;
> and serve him day and night in his temple;
> and the one who sits on the throne
> will spread his tabernacle over them.
> They will hunger no longer, and thirst no more,
> nor will the sun beat down on them,
> nor any heat.
> For the Lamb in the center of the throne will be their shepherd,
> and will guide them to springs of the water of life;
> and God will wipe away every tear from their eyes."

9–12

Remember, John hears about the Lion and sees the Lamb, two visual images of Jesus (5:5–6). In scene six, John hears about the 144,000 and sees a great multitude, two visual images of the church (7:1–12). The militant church is prepared for battle on earth. The triumphant church, the great multitude, is the church in heaven. The martyrs under the altar are given white robes (6:11), to wait until they are told their numbers are completed. For the martyrs, wearing their robes of white (7:9), now their numbers are complete. They praise God and the Lamb reigning through all eternity. Palm branches recall the crowds in Jerusalem at Jesus's triumphant entry.

In all the New Testament, only Revelation and John's gospel mention the palm branches. This scene and the next continue the heavenly scenes of the one sitting on the throne and the Lamb, the twenty-four elders and the four living creatures. Again, all the angels fall on their faces in worship, a position of humility and vulnerability to honor a far greater power (4:10). The Salvation Hymn (7:10) defies the Roman emperor's claim to be the world's savior. The Lamb alone is Savior! A sevenfold blessing replaces wisdom (5:12) with thanksgiving. Give thanks to the Lamb!

13–14

These are the martyrs, their blood shed in faithfulness to the Lamb. Revelation anticipates great suffering. The Greek may be translated as suffering, distress, trouble, tribulation, or affliction. Christians endured suffering because of their faith and refused to give the emperor the honor and worship due only to God and the Lamb. Sporadic persecution occurred under Roman emperors over several centuries until Emperor Constantine declared religious tolerance for Christians in AD 313. Assuming Revelation is written in the late 70s, the suffering to come during the reign of Domitian (AD 81–96) is drawing near.

15–17

After suffering and death, they serve God under protection of his heavenly tent. The sun no longer beats down on them (Psalm 121:5). They hunger and thirst no longer. The Lamb, also the Good Shepherd (Psalm 23; Isaiah 40:11), leads by springs of the water of life (Psalm 36:8–9) and wipes every tear from their eyes (Isaiah 25:8). Seeing the worship in this heavenly scene, imagine praises on earth in pastures, green. All God's people join with heart and voice, in one accord to gather before the throne and rejoice.

Come, all you believers. Join in song. All living creatures, now sing along. Taste the grace of sins forgiven. Celebrate the joy of living. Scene six draws to a close.

Scene 7: Silence in Heaven (8:1–2)

When he opened the seventh seal, there was silence in heaven for about half an hour. And I saw the seven angels who stand before God; and they were given seven trumpets.

1–2

With the seventh seal opened, praises in heaven fall silent. There's a dramatic pause before the next scene in the grand drama begins. My soul waits in silence for God only (Psalm 62:1). There will be silence before you, O God (Psalm 65:1). But the Lord is in his holy temple. Let all the earth be silent before him (Habakkuk 2:20). A heavenly scene continues as seven angels receive seven trumpets. In conquest of Jericho (Joshua 6), seven priests with seven trumpets march around the city for seven days. People keep silent until they shout and the walls come tumbling down (Joshua 6:10). With the appearance of the seven angels, the curtain falls on act II.

To summarize Revelation up to this point:

- Act I: Jesus walks among the churches. Seven scenes follow with Jesus's messages to seven churches in Asia Minor. (This is the present age that John describes as *what is*.)
- Act II: Visions of God's heavenly throne room set the stage for the four horsemen that picture war, violence, and chaos sounding much like two events in the years prior to John's visions: Christians suffering under the emperor Nero and the siege, fall, and utter destruction of Jerusalem.

Scene five shows the souls of the Christian martyrs, many of whom die during Nero's reign, who cry out to God for justice, praying for vengeance against their persecutors. "How long, O Lord? How long?" (Scenes one through five are set in the present age.)

Scene six pictures a coming day of reckoning, a terrible day of judgment for all evildoers. The symbolism of scene six can be viewed as a step into a time of transition and judgment beyond the plane of human history. After portraying a day of reckoning, scene six continues with visions of the militant church on earth and the triumphant church in heaven.

Scene seven opens with silence, a pause for silent worship, a time-out to set the stage for act III to begin.

ACT III

Stage Setting (8:3–5)

The Golden Altar

Another angel came and stood at the altar, holding a golden censer; and much incense was given to him, to add to the prayers of all the saints on the golden altar before the throne. And the smoke of the incense, with the prayers of the saints, went up before God from the angel's hand. Then the angel took the censer and filled it with the fire from the altar, and threw it to the earth; and thunder rumbled and voices sounded and lightning flashed and then an earthquake.

3–5

Act III lifts the curtain to reveal the heavenly throne room. The furnishings on stage suggest the earthly tabernacle that models the heavenly (Exodus 26:30; Hebrews 8:4–5). The golden altar in the tabernacle stood just outside the veil that separated the Holy of Holies from the Holy Place. Once a year, the high priest took the blood of sacrifice, incense, and coals from the golden altar into the Holy of Holies to make atonement for sin. He threw incense on the hot coals, and a cloud of incense ascended to cover the mercy seat (Exodus 25:17–22; Leviticus 16:11–14), a scene that Jewish Christians understood.

The martyrs under the altar have cried cry out for justice (6:9–11). The angel appears to take the high priest's place of intercession, but as Jesus is our High Priest and intercessor (Hebrews 4:14–15), the angel's role is to demonstrate that God has already heard and will respond to their prayers. Given white robes, they are told to wait a while until joined by others who are also to be killed (6:9–11). Later that number of martyrs will encompass a great multitude (7:9).

The prayers of the saints, combined with the smoke of the incense, ascend to God (Psalm 141:2). In anticipation of this scene, the saints' prayers were identified earlier with the incense (5:8). The literal meaning of this word "saints" is "holy ones." All Christians were known as saints in the early church, called to be set apart, to be made holy for God's service. The fire of the altar is thrown upon the earth. God hears their prayers! The thunder rumbles, voices sound, lightning flashes (4:6), and an earthquake follows. Warning! Danger! Stay back! Be ready for act III to begin!

ACT III

The Seven Trumpets
(8:6–11:18)

Scene One: The Plague of Hail and Fire (8:6–7)

And the seven angels who had the seven trumpets prepared to sound them. The first sounded, and there came hail and fire, mixed with blood, and this was thrown to the earth; and a third of earth was burned up, and a third of the trees were burned up, and all the green grass was burned up.

6–7

In Act I, Jesus speaks to seven first-century churches. Act II symbolically pictures the world of those churches. Four scenes of four horsemen portray violence and chaos. Scene five pictures martyrs waiting in heaven. Scene six reminds those who suffer God's justice. A day of reckoning is coming (6:10). Scene seven brings silence in heaven. Act III gives an expanded view of scene six, the day of reckoning, a symbolism of the last days as John sees beyond this age into the mystery that hides the birthing of the new age (Romans 8:18–25). But urgent warnings for repentance are ignored (9:20).

Seven angels stand and receive seven trumpets. In Jericho's conquest, trumpets sound! For the last days, the trumpet sounds (Isaiah 27:12–13; Zephaniah 1:14–16). Jewish Christians know their scriptures and understand intuitively that the seven trumpets announce God's coming justice and judgment.

Angels with trumpets retell the story of Moses and Pharaoh. The trumpet plagues mimic Egyptian plagues and remind the churches of coming deliverance. The plagues began a countdown to freedom for the Israelites who sought freedom from Pharaoh to worship God (Exodus 8:27). The trumpet plagues are a sign of God's deliverance while the Roman emperor seeks to take away their freedom to worship God alone.

For comparisons with the Egyptian plagues, sealing the 144,000 (7:2–3) protects God's people from the trumpet plagues just as the Passover Lamb's blood gave protection from the last Egyptian plague, the death of the firstborn (Exodus 12:7–13). The first trumpet announces hail and fire (lightning) mixed with blood. The first plague against Pharaoh turns water into blood (Exodus 7:14–25). Hail and fire fell on Egypt (Exodus 9:23–26). In Revelation, blood is mixed with hail and fire in a fierce storm as rain seems to become blood. God is the victor over Pharaoh; the Lamb is the victor over the emperor. Worthy is the Lamb that was slain!

Scene Two: The Plague of Blood (8:8–9)

The second angel sounded, and something like a great mountain burning with fire was thrown into the sea; and a third of the sea became blood, and a third of the living creatures in the sea, died; and a third of the ships were destroyed.

8–9

The second trumpet sounds. Another scene begins. Blood is a reoccurring theme. The Lamb's blood points the way to salvation, but blood throughout Revelation also becomes a symbol of judgment. Fire and blood appear in this second plague. A great mountain of fire turns a third of the sea to blood. The drama of the plagues aims to create an emotional response leading to repentance. The trumpet plagues picture a third of nearly everything being destroyed, a threat increased from earlier destruction, which amounted to a fourth (6:7–8).

The plagues are symbols of God's judgment. They are warnings of the calamity sure to fall upon those who continue to do evil. But judgment is still held back. God's goal always aims for justice and salvation, not destruction.

Scene Three: The Plague of Bitterness (8:10–11)

The third angel sounded, and a great star, burning like a torch, fell from heaven, and it fell on a third of the rivers and on the springs of water. The star's name is Wormwood; and a third of the waters became wormwood, and many people died from the waters because they were made bitter.

10–11

These scenes pass quickly from one to another. The third angel sounds the trumpet, and a great burning star strikes the earth. The burning mountain of scene two and the burning star of scene three are both descriptions of meteorites. These were frightful events in ancient society, interpreted as signs of God's wrath. Wormwood is a name for a bitter, poisonous plant (Deuteronomy 2:18). It's a metaphor for bitterness (Proverbs 5:3–5; Amos 6:12). Wormwood makes the water unfit to drink. This plague of poisoned water is much like the first Egyptian plague of water turned to blood (Exodus 7:20).

Scene Four: The Plague of Darkness (8:12–13)

The fourth angel sounded, and a third of the sun and a third of the moon and a third of the stars were struck, so that a third of them were darkened and a third of the day would not have light, and likewise the night. Then I looked, and heard an angel flying in midheaven, crying out with a loud voice, "Woe, woe, woe to those who dwell on the earth, because of the remaining blasts of the trumpet about to be sounded by the three angels!"

12–13

The fourth trumpet sounds; another scene quickly appears. Each plague is directed toward nature. This one strikes a third of the sun, moon, and stars with darkness. It's also symbolic of human beings blindly walking in moral and spiritual darkness (John 1:5). Likely an eclipse, it's comparable to the plague of darkness (Exodus 10:21–23). Prophets warned of events in the heavens as signs of God's judgment (Amos 8:9; Isaiah 13:10; Mark 13:24) and coming darkness and gloom (Joel 2:2).

The flying eagle in mid-heaven, visible to the earth, has a message for all to see and hear. This message of woe is a transition from the first four plagues to the last three. Three woes are for an emphasis on the severity of the coming judgment. The next plagues are to fall more directly on human beings.

Scene Five: The Plague of Super Locusts (9:1–12)

And the fifth angel sounded, and I saw a star from heaven which had fallen to the earth; and the key to the bottomless pit was given to him. When he opened the bottomless pit; smoke went up out of the pit, like smoke of a great furnace; and the sun and the air were darkened by the smoke of the pit. And from the smoke came locusts upon the earth; and authority was given them, like that of the scorpions of the earth. They were told not to hurt the grass of the earth, nor any green thing, nor any tree, but only the people who do not have the seal of God on their foreheads. And they were not permitted to kill anyone, but to torment them for five months; and their torment was like when a scorpion stings a person. In those days, people will seek death but will not find it; and they will long to die and death will flee from them.

In appearance, the locusts were like horses prepared for battle; they wore on their heads, what appeared to be crowns of gold, and their faces were like human faces. They had hair like women's hair and their teeth were like lion's teeth. And they had scales like breastplates of iron; and the sound of their wings was like the sound of many horses and chariots rushing into battle. And they had tails with stingers, like scorpions; and their power to hurt people for five months is in their tails. They have as king over them, the angel of the abyss; his name in Hebrew is Abaddon, and in Greek, his name is Apollyon. The first woe is past; look, two woes are still coming after these things

1–6

The bottomless pit, the abyss (9:11, 20:1, Luke 8:31; Romans 10:7), means the underworld, under the earth (5:3, 5:13), known as Sheol by the Hebrews and Hades by the Greeks. This refers to the ancient world view of the dead as departed spirits under the earth. The fallen star is an angel carrying out God's will (20:1). The smoke of a great furnace alludes to God's awesome appearance at Mt. Sinai (Exodus 19:18) and the destruction of Sodom and Gomorrah (Genesis 19:28).

These terribly destructive insects breed in desert areas and descend on any vegetation like an invading army. These are not cicadas (also called locusts), but the locusts are known also as grasshoppers. A locust swarm may be a hundred feet wide, four miles long, eating everything in its path. Locusts continue the symbolism of the Egyptian plagues against Pharaoh (Exodus 10:12–20).

But there's a cruel twist to the locust story: These gluttonous super insects do not eat vegetation but have tails like scorpions to torture people with their stings. A locust plague would darken the sky as does the smoke, a double whammy. Those sealed by God on their foreheads are assured of escaping this predicted torment (7:3). A warning of seeking death and being unable to find it is found in Job 3:21. Scorpions, like locusts, are commonly found in the deserts of the Middle East. Their sting is painful but not fatal.

7–12

John draws comparisons with the locust plague in Joel. They have an appearance like horses (Joel 2:4) and teeth like lions (Joel 1:6). Five is a symbolic number, half of ten (a whole number). Five is also symbolic of a limited time. And five months is also the maximum life span of locusts.

The angel of the abyss is Abaddon. The deepest part of the abyss is called Abaddon. Abaddon is a name for Sheol (Job 26:6) and is paired with death (Job 28:22). It means destruction. The Greek name Apollyon is a possible sarcastic reference to the Greek god, Apollo. The plagues threaten destruction, but God's goal is repentance. Temporary misery mercifully offers time for repentance. An abyss also lies within the human heart. Evil can emerge and lead to destruction and unspeakable horror. The heart is deceitful and fearfully wicked (Jeremiah 17:9).

The sounding of the fifth trumpet is a warning to flee sin and its consequences. This first of three woes enforces the warning: Don't wait any longer. Seek repentance. These symbols of destruction are only to become more and more hideous. The time for repentance is now. Two more woes are to come. Stay tuned!

Scene Six: The Plague of Demonic Calvary (9:13–21)

The sixth angel sounded, and I heard a voice from the four horns of the golden altar which is before God. It said to the sixth angel who had the trumpet, "Release the four angels who are bound at the great river Euphrates." And the four angels, who had been prepared for this very hour and day and month and year, were released, to kill a third of humankind. And the number of the armies of the horsemen was twice ten thousand times ten thousand; I heard the number. I saw like this, the vision of the horses and those who sat on them: they had breastplates the color of fire and of hyacinth and of brimstone; the heads of the horses looked like heads of lions; and fire and smoke and brimstone came out of their mouths. A third of humankind was killed by the three plagues of fire and smoke and brimstone that came out of their mouths. The power of the horses was in their mouths and in their tails; their tails were like serpents with heads and with them they wound.

The rest of humankind, who were not killed by these plagues, did not repent of the works of their hands; nor did they stop worshiping demons, and idols made of gold and silver and brass and stone and wood, which can neither see, hear nor walk; and they did not repent of their murders nor of their sorceries nor of their immorality nor of their thefts.

13–19

The scene changes. The sounding of the sixth trumpet releases four angels bound at the Euphrates River. Rome's first-century empire extended to the Euphrates in the east where the armies of Parthia posed a constant threat to invade Rome. The Parthian Empire, including today's Iran and Iraq, reached east to China. Thoughts of a Parthian invasion struck terror in many Roman citizens. But for persecuted Christians and others subject to Rome's brutality, a Roman defeat would bring hope of new freedom. The first four trumpets warned of destruction to nature. The fifth trumpet warned of suffering, but not death, to humankind. With the sounding of the sixth trumpet comes a warning that a third of people are to be killed.

In the Greek, the number is two myriad myriads. A myriad is ten thousand. The number is twice ten thousand times ten thousand. John's source for the number is Psalm 68:17. The horsemen are more demonic than flesh and blood. Fire, smoke, and brimstone come from the horses' mouths. The destruction of Sodom and Gomorrah provides imagery to reinforce the warning (Genesis 19:24–28). No biblical source exists for horses with tails like serpents. John specifically says he received a vision.

20–21

But there is no repentance for demon worship (Deuteronomy 32:17; Psalm 106:37), idol worship (Psalm 115:4–7; Daniel 5:23), or crimes against each other. The broken relationships with God lead to broken relationships with our fellow human beings. With the breaking of the first seal (6:1–2), a leader (Rome) of a conquering army brings destruction to the earth's inhabitants. The sixth trumpet warns of a dreaded foe (Parthia). What goes around comes around. God allows humans the freedom to slaughter one another. Idol worship is humanity's fundamental sin. Turn away from worship of the true God, and all other sins follow (Exodus 20:1–17). The plagues' horrid symbolism is meant to bring repentance. Still no sign of repentance is yet seen coming. How long, O God? How long?

Scene Six Continued: The Angel with the Little Scroll (10:1–11)

And I saw another mighty angel coming down out of heaven, clothed with a cloud, a rainbow upon his head, his face like the sun, and his legs like pillars of fire; and he held in his hands a little scroll which was open. And he placed his right foot on the sea and his left on the land; and he cried out with a loud voice, like a lion's roar; when he had cried out, the seven peals of thunder uttered their voices. And when the seven peals of thunder had spoken, and I was about to write; I heard a voice from heaven saying, "Seal up the things which the seven peals of thunder have spoken, and do not write them." Then the angel I saw, standing on the sea and on the land,

> raised his right hand to heaven;
> and swore by him who lives forever and ever,

who created heaven and the things in it, the earth and the things in it, and the sea and the things in it, that there shall be no more delay, but in the days of the voice of the seventh angel, which he is about to sound, then the mystery of God is finished, as he preached to his servants the prophets.

And the voice which I heard speaking from heaven, I again heard speaking to me, and saying, "Go take the scroll which is open in the hand of the angel who stands on the sea and on the land." And I went to the angel, telling him to give me the little scroll. And he said to me, "Take it, and eat it; and it will make your stomach bitter, but in your mouth, it will be sweet as honey." And I took the little scroll out of the angel's hand and ate it; in my mouth it was sweet as honey, and when I had eaten it, my stomach was made bitter. And they said to me, "You must prophesy again about many peoples and nations and tongues and kings."

1–3

Scene six is greatly expanded, as is scene six of the seven seals. Another mighty angel appears. The first mighty angel searched for the one who was worthy to open the scroll with its seven seals (5:2). This second mighty angel holds that same scroll, now open. A slightly different Greek word is used here, which is translated as "little scroll." It's the same scroll. Both Revelation 5:1 and 10:2 depend on Ezekiel 2–3. Revelation 5:1 depends on Ezekiel 2:10. Later Revelation 10:8–11 depends on Ezekiel 3:1–3.[9]

Remember, the seven visions, which accompany the opening of the scroll's seven seals (6–8), are not the scroll's actual contents. As the scroll is finally open, the suspense continues to build. Since 5:1, the audience has been waiting for the scroll's message to be revealed, and at last the time is drawing near. After the plagues against Pharaoh, God led the people out of Egypt by a pillar of cloud by day and a pillar of fire by night (Exodus 13:21). The cloud and fire are symbols of God's presence and guiding hand amidst suffering.

The angel straddles sea and land, indicating God's rule and authority over all creation. His stance also shows that God is far greater than the sea and land beasts soon to be introduced (13:1–18). God will be more than a match for any two beasts from the pit of Hades. The angel cries out with a loud voice, like a lion's roar (Amos 3:7–8). The seven peals of thunder are an allusion to the seven descriptions of God's thunder-like voice found in Psalm 29. Revelation, like the psalm, calls the faithful to worship God, who is King over the world, for already Satan's doom is sure and God's people will endure. And above all earthly powers, God alone over the world rules. Worthy alone is God and the Lamb! Worthy!

4–7

John is told not to write the content of the seven voices of thunder because there will be no more delay. God sees that nothing will change even if the seven thunders are to announce greater calamities. Going back to 9:21, there was no repentance after the seven seals or seven trumpets. The seals herald suffering to come upon a fourth of the earth (6:8). Then the trumpets announce that suffering is coming to a third of the earth (8:7, 8–9, 10–11, 12, 15); but neither seals or trumpets are sufficient to bring repentance. It's time to move on. The time for delay is over.

But as happens again and again, there is more still to be revealed. Judgment will be held back before any conclusion is reached. It looks like time for the seventh angel to blow his trumpet, but not yet. In due time, when the trumpet blows, the mystery will be made known to his servants, the prophets (Amos 3:6–7).

In both act II and III, an extra-long sixth scene helps build the suspense ahead of the seventh scene. In verse two, the strong angel has the little scroll. We have discovered it is the same scroll that only the lamb was found worthy to open (5:2–6). Worthy is the Lamb that was slain. The Lamb of God, the Holy Lamb of God! Now with the scroll open, we are closer than ever to discovering its message.

8–11

John does as he is told and takes the scroll from the angel's hand. This sequence (1:1) from God (5:10), Jesus (5:7), an angel (10:2), and John (10:10) is finally completed as John receives the scroll. And like the prophet Ezekiel, John will eat the scroll (Ezekiel 3:1–3). When Ezekiel eats the scroll, it tastes sweet. John is told the scroll will be sweet as honey in his mouth but will be bitter in his stomach. John eats the scroll and finds this to be true. God's word may taste sweet, but it may become bitter when digested, and the truth must be proclaimed. As he speaks the words of the scroll, this becomes a prophecy for many peoples, nations, kings, and tongues to hear. The prophecy, the scroll's message, is about to be revealed at the turn of a page! The suspense builds!

Scene Six Continued: Measuring the Temple (11:1–2)

I was given a measuring rod like a staff; and was told, "Rise and measure the temple of God, and the altar, and those who worship there, but do not measure the court outside the temple; leave that out, for it is given over to the nations, and they will trample the holy city for forty-two months."

1

With a measuring rod, John begins to reveal the scroll's contents. We have waited for this moment since the Lamb received the scroll (5:7) This measuring of the temple has a parallel in Ezekiel 40:3 and Zechariah 2:1. The Romans have already destroyed Jerusalem's temple. The temple John measures is the church (1 Corinthians 3:16, 6:19). He goes on to measure the altar and those who worship in the temple (Revelation 21:9–15). As suffering appears on the horizon (Jeremiah 12:5), are the churches ready to fulfill their mission? Now the open scroll has found its voice. Its words are telling the churches: measure yourself carefully (Romans 5:1–5). How do you measure up? How would we measure up in the face of such suffering? What will be the tale of the tape?

2

The outer court of the Jerusalem temple was known as the Court of the Gentiles. This was the court for so-called God-fearers, those attracted to the Jewish faith but not yet ready to convert. Why not measure the outer court? For Christians, no middle ground exists when suffering comes. Those on the fence, unwilling to fully commit to Christ (outer court), are not measured. They cannot be counted on when suffering comes, when those come who will "trample" the faith underfoot. Forty-two months, three and a half years, 1,260 days, a time, times, and half a time, all these refer to half of seven (three and a half). Seven is the number for completion, for wholeness. While half of seven is a limited amount of time, a symbolic number, it's also the length of time the Jews suffered under the Syrian ruler, Antiochus IV (167–164 BC). He placed an altar to Zeus in the temple, the abomination of desolation (Daniel 12:5–13). Judas Maccabeus led the Jewish revolt that followed; the invaders were defeated in 164 BC. The pagan altar was destroyed, and the temple was reconsecrated. Three and a half years is the approximate time of the siege of Jerusalem of which Jesus warned (Mark 13:14). The city fell to the Romans in AD 70.

Scene Six Continued: Two Witnesses (11:3–14)

"And I will enable my two witnesses to prophesy for one thousand two hundred sixty days, clothed in sackcloth." These are the two olive trees and the two lampstands that stand before the Lord of the earth. If anyone attempts to harm them, fire comes out of their mouths, and devours their enemies; and anyone who wants to harm them, in this manner must be killed. These have the power to shut up the sky, so rain will not fall during the days of their prophesying; and they have power to turn the waters into blood, and to strike the earth with every plague, as often as they want.

And when they have finished their testimony, the beast that comes up out of the abyss will attack them, and overcome them and kill them. And their dead bodies will lie in the street of the great city which figuratively is called Sodom and Egypt, where also their Lord was crucified. And some from all peoples and tribes and tongues and nations will look on their dead bodies for three and a half days, and not permit them to be laid in a tomb. And the earth's inhabitants will rejoice over them and celebrate and exchange gifts with one another, because these two prophets tormented the inhabitants of the earth.

But after three and a half days, the breath of life from God came into them, and they stood on their feet; and great terror fell upon those who looked on them. And they heard a loud voice from heaven saying to them, "Come up here." And they went up into heaven in the cloud, while their enemies looked on. And at that hour there was a severe earthquake, and a tenth of the city fell; and seven thousand people were killed in the earthquake, and the rest were terrified and gave glory to the God of heaven. The second woe is past; look, the third woe is coming quickly.

3–6

The two witnesses are two lampstands and two olive trees (Zechariah 4:1–14). The lampstands are symbols of the churches' witness (Matthew 5:14–16). Two witnesses are needed to confirm the truth (Deuteronomy 19:15). Sackcloth symbolizes the repentance needed for the church's witness to be effective, a need made clear in the messages to the seven churches. The churches receive a time to witness of 1,260 days, the same time found in verse two (three and a half years). It's a limited time to witness to the word of God and testimony of Jesus Christ. The church is the new Israel, empowered by the Spirit (Zechariah 4:6).

For the context of the fire that devours its enemies, read 2 Kings 1. Elijah speaks, and fire comes down from heaven, not literally from his mouth, but from his words. This also explains a New Testament scripture (Luke 9:54). The image of "shutting up the sky" also comes from Elijah (1 Kings 17–18). Water turned to blood, and other plagues are allusions to Moses and the plagues against Pharaoh (including Exodus 7:17–20). Moses and Elijah are symbols for the church's witness.

7–10

The witnesses' testimony is complete! The churches remain faithful, even to death, faithful to the Word of God and the testimony of Jesus Christ! They are killed by the beast from the abyss who appears later as the beast from the sea (13:7). The great city, where the bodies of the witnesses lie, is a city of sin (Sodom) and slavery (Egypt). The city where their Lord was crucified need not be Jerusalem because he overcomes wherever sin and slavery rule. The great city, likely Rome (18:10–21), may be any city where God's people bear witness to the point of giving up their lives. In any city in which they are killed, they witness, even in death, to the gospel of Jesus Christ. Their dead bodies lie unburied (Psalm 79:1–3). Three and a half as half of seven, the complete number, again indicates a limited time and may also represent Jesus's time in the tomb. Low in the grave Jesus lay, from where he emerged in victory!

11–14

Some may be relieved when their sins seem hidden and rejoice over the witness's death. Three and a half days is the limited time mentioned in verse 9. After death, they stand on their feet, an allusion to Ezekiel 37:1–10. As Ezekiel prophesies over Israel's many dry bones, they take on flesh and skin. He prophesies to the Breath (Spirit), and the slain ones live and stand up. Through the Spirit and the blood of the martyrs, the church is raised up and lives again. Their enemies can only watch a triumphant church raised up from harm's way. The martyrs receive their reward, joining the triumphant church in heaven (7:13–17).

A great earthquake, a symbol of God's judgment, is tempered with mercy. A tenth appears in scripture as a remnant saved (Isaiah 6:13).

The seven thousand suggests the remnant who did not bow to Baal in 1 Kings 19:18. But grace abounds, and only a tenth, a reversal of the remnant, is lost.[10] The rest is saved! They are terrified, in true fear (awe) of the Lord, and give glory to God, a true sign of repentance, unlike in 9:21.

The scroll's message is revealed at last: Through their own faithful witness even to death, God's people help bring the nations to repentance and faith.[11] The saint's witness becomes a deciding factor for those who are saved and give glory to God! We would remain true always to Jesus, for there are those who need our witness! The Lamb's followers have been redeemed from all the nations (5:9) so they may witness to all the nations (11:3–13).[12]

Scene Seven: Loud Voices in Heaven (11:15-17)

Then the seventh angel sounded; and there were loud voices from heaven, saying,

> "The kingdom of the world has become the
>   kingdom of our Lord and of his Christ;
>   and he shall reign forever and ever.

And the twenty-four elders who set on their thrones before God fell on their faces and worshiped God, saying,

> "We give you thanks, O Lord God, the Almighty,
>   who are and who were, because you have taken
>   your great power and begun to reign."

15-17

It's a scene of triumph; the Lord God is victorious! Voices in heaven lift their praises. The Lord shall reign forever and ever (Exodus 15). The twenty-four elders fall in worship. We give you thanks, O Lord God, there is no one like you, O Lord! God no longer is the one who is to come. God is here! Awesome in wonders! Majestic in holiness! The source of inspiration for the Halleluiah chorus! The kingdom of this world is to become the kingdom of our Lord and of his Christ. The Lamb's role is to establish God's kingdom on earth to replace the kingdom of the world. All earthly kingdoms are lumped together as one. None compares to the coming kingdom of God. Revelation embodies these three petitions of the Lord's prayer:

- Hallowed be Thy Name (4:11–5:14)
- Thy kingdom come (11:15–17)
- Thy will be done on earth as in heaven (21:1–22:5)

It's a celebration! The Lamb's reign has begun! This seems to be a climax to the entire first half of Revelation. However, it is important to remember all events are not necessarily in order.

Scene Seven Continued: A Preview of Coming Attractions (11:18)

And the nations raged,
and your anger came,
and the time came for the dead to be judged,
and to reward your bond-servants the prophets and the saints
and those who fear your name,
the small and great,
and to destroy those who destroy the earth.

18

This verse takes a step back and appears much like a summary, some of it inspired by Psalm 2, of what's ahead in act IV (12:1–15:4).

1. 12–13: Compare Psalm 2:1–3 (the nations were enraged).
2. 14:1–5: Compare Psalm 2:6: I have installed My King upon Zion.

3. 14:6–11: Compare Psalm 2:12 (and your wrath came).
4. 14:14–20: (and the time came for the dead to be judged).
5. 15:1–4: (and the time to reward your bond-servants …).

With verse 18, the curtain falls, closing act III and completing the first half of Revelation. Act III is followed by an intermission before the drama will resume with Act IV. Take time to stand up, stretch your legs, and be prepared to follow the next acts of this amazing first-century drama. Below is a summary of what you have seen so far:

- Act I: The seven messages of Jesus to the seven churches.
- Act II: The seven seals. The seals are being opened, but the scroll's content can only be revealed when all the seals are opened. The first four openings are accompanied by scenes that picture the world of the seven churches that look much like events in the Roman Empire during AD 60s and 70s. Scene five shows the martyrs in heaven crying out for vengeance on their enemies, and scene six gives warning of the day of reckoning coming. The scene continues with an interlude, showing the militant and then the triumphant church. Scene 7 concludes act II with a time of silent worship in heaven.
- Act III: This entire act represents a more expansive picture of the day of reckoning introduced in Act II. A trumpet is sounded to open each scene. The first six trumpets sound the warnings of the reckoning to follow (Isaiah 2:12–22). But these dire warnings show no sign of leading the nations to repentance. The sixth scene continues with a long interlude after the sixth trumpet. During this time, the contents of the scroll, which was unsealed in act II, are beginning to be revealed as John eats the unsealed scroll. He eats the scroll and proclaims the scroll's contents, which show the martyrs' witness to the Lamb are moving the nations to repentance

and faith. Then the seventh trumpet sounds to celebrate the Lamb's reign, and the drama looks ahead to act IV. But first, the intermission comes about halfway through the drama. Three acts have been completed with four more to go. Hang on to your hats.

ACT IV

Stage Setting (11:19)

The Ark of the Covenant

And God's temple in heaven was opened, and the ark of his covenant appeared in his temple, and lightning flashed and voices sounded and thunder rumbled, then an earthquake and a great hailstorm.

19

The stage setting for act IV is the open temple of God in heaven with the ark of the covenant visible. It's as if God has pulled back the curtain of heaven, as when Jesus died on the cross and the veil of the temple was turned asunder, top to bottom (Mark 15:37–38). God's people receive direct access to the throne. God alone is King! Awesome God! Creator of the visible and invisible, countless stars, galaxies, black holes, dark matter, and dark energy, farthest reaches of time and space, and precious jewel of Planet Earth! God's power, majesty, and holiness are expressed with lightning flashes, thunder crashes, and an earthquake. And then a great hailstorm is added. Awesome God! Our God is an awesome God! The Lord God, omnipotent reigns! God shall reign forever and ever and ever! All wisdom, power, and love belong to the Lord God above. Our Creator, Redeemer, and friend promises to be with us to the end. It's only with grace we can run the race. Give thanks with grateful hearts!

ACT IV

The Seven Insights (12:1–15:4)

Scene One: The Radiant Woman and the Red Dragon (12:1–17)

Then a great sign appeared in heaven, a woman clothed with the sun, the moon under her feet and wearing a crown of twelve stars on her head. She was with child. And being in labor to give birth, she cried out in pain. Another sign appeared in heaven, a great fiery red dragon with seven heads and ten horns, with seven crowns on his heads. And his tail swept away a third of the stars of heaven, and threw them to the earth. Then the dragon stood before the woman who was about to give birth, ready to devour her child at birth. And she gave birth to a son, who is to shepherd all the nations with a rod of iron; and her child was caught up to God, to his throne. Then the woman fled into the wilderness, where she has a place prepared by God, so there she would be nourished for one thousand two hundred sixty days.

War occurred in heaven, Michael and his angels fighting the dragon. And the dragon and his angels fighting back. But they were not strong enough, and there was no longer a place for them in heaven. And the great dragon was thrown down, the serpent of old who is called the devil and Satan, who deceives the whole world; he was thrown down to the earth, and his angels were thrown down with him. And I heard a loud voice in heaven, saying,

> "Now the salvation, and the power,
> and the kingdom of our God
> and the authority of his Christ have come,
> for the accuser of our brothers and sisters has been thrown down,
> who accuses them before our God day and night.
> And they overcame him through the blood of the Lamb
> and through the word of their testimony,
> and they did not love their life even to death.
> Therefore rejoice, O heavens and all who dwell in them.
> Woe to the earth and the sea, because the
> devil has come down to you
> with great fury,
> knowing that his time is short."

And when the dragon saw that he was thrown down to the earth, he pursued the woman who gave birth to the baby boy. But the woman was given the two wings of the great eagle, so that she could fly into the wilderness to her place, where she was nourished from the presence of the serpent for a time and times and half a time. Then the serpent poured water like a river out of his mouth after the woman, so he might sweep her away with the flood. But the earth helped the woman, and the earth opened its mouth and drank up the river that the dragon poured out of his mouth. And the dragon was enraged with the woman, and went off to make war with the rest of her offspring, who keep the commandments of God and hold to the testimony of Jesus.

1–3

Up to now, Revelation says little about an ages-long war between God and the evil powers that challenge his reign over the world.

In act I, the churches are urged to overcome. The stage is set in act II with the throne room of God and the Lamb who has overcome. Now after act III, act IV reveals the identity of the one whom the Lamb has overcome and whom God's people must overcome. It's God's principal enemy, the unholy trinity, the vile opposite of the Holy Trinity.

But first the radiant woman enters the stage. Who is she? The sun, moon, and twelve stars suggest Joseph's dream in Genesis 37:9. Joseph was God's instrument for saving his family, keeping a people alive to become a nation. The radiant woman is the people of God. She is Israel, who is about to give birth to the Messiah (Isaiah 26:17). And as the people of God, she is also the church. Another sign appears, the great red dragon.

Look ahead to verse 9 where his identity is revealed. This dragon-adversary of God appears to be that mythical sea monster, Leviathan (Job 3:8; Psalm 104:26; Isaiah 27:1). The Bible does not number Leviathan's heads (Psalm 74:14). Leviathan lives in the sea and creates chaos. God subdues cosmic powers to bring order to the chaos, often represented by waters of the sea (Genesis 1:2).

When the new heaven and new earth comes, there is no more sea (21:1). It's the end of this chaos monster. Seven heads label the dragon as totally evil. The horn is a symbol of power. Ten is a round number for the lesser powers that follow the dragon (Daniel 7:7).

4–6

The dragon is the first of an evil threesome introduced in act IV. The dragon's war with the woman is the first of seven insights into the battle raging between good and evil. The dragon brings down stars, perhaps fallen angels, to earth with his tail (Daniel 8:10) and prepares to devour the child. He tried through Herod (Matthew 2) and then the cross (John 12:31–32), but the evil one is not powerful enough. The woman (Israel) gives birth to the male child (Isaiah 66:7), the Messiah who will shepherd the nations with a rod of iron (Psalm 2:9).

The rod is a stout club-like stick with iron attached to one end. Shepherds used it to defend their sheep and themselves from robbers and wild animals. Jesus's birth and ascension (caught up to God) goes as planned. Heaven is a higher dimension (Isaiah 55:9). In an age of kings, the throne is a symbol of authority and rule.

The wilderness is a place of refuge and respite for the woman. The 1,260 days is the same number of three and a half that appears frequently. Here it may represent a limited time before persecution comes.

7–9

The devil and his minions are no match for Michael, the archangel (Jude 9), and his angels. Satan is banished from heaven. Satan is the red dragon in verse three. Jewish sources outside the Old Testament label Satan as a fallen angel, banished from heaven because of pride. He tried to be equal to God. Imagine that. Jesus sees Satan's fall (Luke 10:18). Jesus's death and resurrection dealt the devil a mortal blow but the war is not yet over. WWII, Allied forces won the decisive battle on D-Day, but fighting continued until V-E Day when the war in Europe was finally over.

The Bible hints at an ages-long war between God and evil. What does God at war mean if God is sovereign? Sovereignty is not control of every detail. Both evil spirit beings and human beings are given the ability to make choices. This ability to choose brings them into conflict with God's perfect will.[13] God's sovereignty is proven in battle. God's creation is good, but rebellious forces threaten a good creation with chaos, symbolized by the red dragon thrown down to earth. God overcomes chaos and restores creation.

God's true sovereignty is on display daily in Jesus's life, death, and resurrection. It's a war out there as Jesus faces demonic powers and human opposition. Then at last on Friday, as the sky darkens, a bloody figure hanging on a cross cries out, "It is finished." It looks like all is lost. But the cry from the cross is a victory shout. The sovereign God is victor over all foes. Joyful shouts on Sunday morning, "He is risen," confirming God's triumphant victory! Jesus Christ is risen today!

10–12

This is another salvation hymn (7:10, 19:1). The Roman Empire portrayed itself as the world's savior. These salvation hymns are songs of defiance, public announcements that God alone is Savior. These are the same martyrs who remain faithful even to death (6:9–11). They overcome Satan by the blood of the Lamb and the word of their testimony. They overcome! Their testimony, as martyrs, celebrates the Lordship of Jesus Christ, in defiance of the Roman emperor's pretensions of lordship. By their witness, they aid in the defeat of Satan and his Roman cronies. The martyrs' faithful witness helps defeat the powers of evil.[14]

Satan had been hurled down to earth (Luke 10:18). The heavens rejoice (Isaiah 49:13; Psalm 96:11), but still woes are coming to earth. The name Satan means the adversary, the one who accuses. Satan, the adversary, is the serpent of old (Genesis 3:1) and father of lies (John 8:44). His time is short. His days are numbered because Christ is risen and the kingdom has come. Jesus won the victory on the cross, overcoming all powers of evil. Sing to the Lamb his song of salvation. Let it be heard by every king and nation. There is power in the blood of the Lamb.

13–17

Verse 13 follows verse 9. When is the dragon thrown down to earth? When he is defeated on the cross. That's when Satan's doom is sealed, as Jesus predicted (Luke 10:18). The dragon goes after the woman again. Although the allusions to scripture are about Israel, the woman is the church. Like Israel, the church is also God's own possession. The wings of the great eagle offer the woman sanctuary (Exodus 19:4–6; Deuteronomy 32:11). Time, times, and half time is the same number as three and a half (Daniel 7:25). The earth helps the woman, opens its mouth, and drinks up the river from the dragon's mouth (Exodus 15:12; Isaiah 51:10).

Though the martyrs will go through flood and fire (Isaiah 43:2), their time of suffering will be limited now. These are the same people of God, the same martyrs found in 11:3. Remember Revelation does not proceed on a straight line. It returns again and again to cover the same ground. The martyrs win more victories as they continue to testify. Jesus Christ alone is Lord, and God's glory they magnify. They are committed to keeping the commandments of God and holding to the testimony of Jesus Christ. The accuser is filled with rage and not about to exit the stage. The martyrs declare that Jesus is Lord and win more victories for God. They shall be spared by the raging flood. They shall overcome by the Lamb's blood. They are saved in their darkest hour, for in the blood, there is wondrous power. The old red dragon is enraged. And the saints shall overcome!

Scene Two: The Beast from the Sea (13:1–10)

And he stood on the sand of the seashore. And I saw a beast coming up out of the sea, with ten horns and seven heads, and on its horns, ten diadems, and on its heads, blasphemous names. And the beast which I saw was like a leopard, and its feet were like bear's feet, and its mouth like a lion's mouth. And the dragon gave it its power and its throne and great authority. And one of its heads looked as though it had been slain, and its fatal wound was healed. And the whole earth was amazed and followed the beast; and they worshiped the dragon, because he gave his authority to the beast; and they worshiped the beast, saying, "Who is like the beast, and who is able to wage war with him?

And it was given a mouth speaking arrogant words and blasphemies; and authority to act for forty-two months was given to it. And it opened it mouth in blasphemies against God, to blaspheme his name and his tabernacle, that is, those who dwell in heaven. And it was permitted to make war with the saints and to overcome them; and it was given authority over every tribe and people and tongue and nation. And all who dwell on the earth will worship it, all whose name was not written from the foundation of the world in the book of life of the Lamb who has been slain. If anyone has an ear, let him hear.

> If anyone is destined for captivity,
> to captivity he goes;
> if anyone kills with the sword,
> with the sword he must be killed.

Here is the perseverance and the faith of the saints.

1–4

John is granted a second insight into the ancient battle between good and evil. The beast from the sea is revealed. Like the red dragon, the beast has seven heads and ten horns. As the second member of an unholy trinity, the second one mimics the first. The beast's likeness is to a leopard, a bear, and a lion (Daniel 7:4–6). The beast is the Roman Empire. The beast's wound may be a reference to the Nero myth. After Emperor Nero committed suicide, several legends emerged, which usually took one of two forms: either Nero had not died and was in hiding or Nero would be returning from the dead.

The most widespread myth was that Nero didn't die but had fled to Parthia, and from there, he would return with the huge Parthian army to destroy Rome. But instead of a Nero myth, the fatal wound of the sea beast is more likely a parody of Jesus: a parody of the second member of the Holy Trinity by the beast who is the second member of the unholy trinity.

John saw one of the beast's heads look as if it had been slain (13:3). Similar language is used for Jesus, the Lamb standing as though slain (5:6). It is likely the healed wound of the beast parodies the wounds of Christ and his resurrection from the dead. But it is not the beast, but Jesus who is the victor! The dragon and the beast receive worship due only God and the Lamb. Who is like the beast? This is blaspheming and a mockery of God (Exodus 15:11; Psalm 35:10).

5–9

The heart of Revelation is the worship of God. And to blaspheme is the opposite of worship, it's to excite contempt and hatred against God and God's people. But the beast only has the authority to act for forty-two months, that limited time (12:14). It was given to the beast to overcome the saints. Dominion is given to it (Daniel 7:6). The dragon makes war on the saints (Daniel 7:21). The beast represents the Roman Empire. Humans are given an awesome freedom to choose. This freedom to choose includes making choices of terrible evil, which God doesn't step in to prevent from occurring.

Revelation shares a common theme with the book of Daniel: God's people are ordered to worship a leader who claims to be divine. Daniel pictures miraculous interventions in chapter 3 (three friends cast into the fiery furnace) and chapter 6 (Daniel in lion's den).

But not in Revelation, as God uses the witness of his saints, who are overcome by the beast, to testify Jesus only is Lord! "If anyone has an ear to hear" are words repeated to each of the seven churches, words used by Jesus. The original context in Isaiah 6:8–13 applies here: Those who have ears to hear are those who sincerely want to hear and to understand and respond. But those who resist hearing the truth only become more hardened and refuse to hear. This was true with Isaiah's hearers, Pharaoh, many who heard Jesus, and those who persecuted John's hearers. Who will heed the warning as John warns that God's judgment is coming (Jeremiah 15:2)?

10

There seem to be those who would willingly use violence on behalf of the Lamb. When is violence acceptable? To defend others? To defend ourselves? And what level of violence is acceptable? There may be no easy answers to these difficult questions, but should we ignore Jesus's words in the Sermon on the Mount (Matthew 5:38–39)? Those destined for captivity go to captivity; those who kill with the sword must be killed by the sword. Compare this with Jesus's warning (Matthew 26:52). The entire Revelation is a plea for perseverance and faith in the time of suffering (Romans 5:1–5).

Hold on. This too shall pass. Jesus spoke of our need to persevere in prayer and faith with his parable of the unrighteous judge (Luke 18:1–8). When Jesus comes, will he find faith on the earth? Some bright day we will understand, but for now, Jesus, take my hand. Our precious Lord, I am tired and worn. Take my hand in the darkness and the storm. Precious Lord, please hear my cry, as Satan is saying there's no need to try. When the storms are howling and there seems no place to hide, give us courage, faith, and grace to take all in stride!

Scene Three: The Beast from the Land (13:11–18)

Then I saw another beast coming up out of the earth; and it had two horns like a lamb, and it spoke like a dragon. And it exercises all the authority of the first beast in its presence. And it makes the earth and those who dwell in it to worship the first beast, whose fatal wound was healed. And it performs great signs, and it even makes fire come down out of heaven to the earth in the presence of people. And it deceives those who dwell on the earth because of the signs which it was permitted to perform in the presence of the beast, telling those who dwell on the earth to make an image of the beast who was wounded by the sword and has come to life. And allowed to give breath to the image of the beast, so that the beast's image would even speak and cause those who do not worship the image of the beast to be killed. And it causes all, the small and the great, the rich and the poor, and the free and the slaves, to be marked on their right hand or on their forehead, so no one will be able to buy or sell, except the one who has the mark, of the name of the beast or the number of its name. Here is wisdom. Let him who has understanding calculate the number of the beast, for it is the number for humanity; and its number is six hundred sixty-six.

11–15

Scene three introduces John's third insight into the battle between good and evil. It's the beast from the earth who masquerades as a lamb but speaks as a dragon. This third member of the unholy trinity is the classic wolf in sheep's clothing. This evil deceiver, this master of the lie, represents the Roman bureaucracy that enforced emperor worship. It exercises all the authority of the second beast (the Roman State). The beast from the earth comes equipped with a pack of lies and its cheap parodies of the truth. The fire from heaven appears to be either a parody of the Holy Spirit at Pentecost or a parody of Elijah (1 Kings 18:38–39; 2 Kings 1:10–14). These great signs are likely a parody of signs performed in the early church (Acts 2:43). The beast from the land continues his parody of the Spirit, as it gives breath to the image of the beast from the sea. This activity is a parody of God breathing life into man (Adam) who is made in

God's image (Genesis 1:26, 2:7). Those who do not fall for the lies and refuse to worship the beast are to be killed.

16–17

A mark on the right hand or forehead is a parody of sealing the 144,000 in chapter 7, those who are saved from God's wrath (6:12–17). These from all walks of life receive a mark to protect them from the empire's wrath, which falls on those who refuse to worship the emperor. If this indeed is parody, likely no actual mark exists. However, the mark suggests a commercial connection to the business and trade associations, in which membership was important for earning a livelihood. Through this participation in the economic life of the empire, Christians were confronted with the practice of eating meat sacrificed to idols. Refusing to participate in such idolatrous rites brought severe economic hardship. And this is what appears to be the mark of the beast.

18

The number 666 gets more attention than it deserves. It's the number for man. The Greek word can mean humankind. It's translated here as "humanity." Having no definite article, it's the number for man, and not the number for *the* man. Therefore, it likely does not refer to a specific individual. In the number scheme of Revelation, six falls one short of seven, the complete number. And six as a symbol for evil represents sinful man, fallen humanity. The number six when repeated three times is 666, the number for sinful humanity under the influence of the unholy trinity. The number seven, if repeated three times, is 777, a number for the Holy Trinity and the redeemed of the Lamb. God called us from our fallen state and adopted us as his children (Ephesians 1:4–8). Amazing grace! How sweet it is!

Scene Four: The Lamb and 144,000 (14:1–5)

I looked and saw, standing on Mt. Zion, the Lamb and with him one hundred forty-four thousand having his name and his Father's name written on their foreheads. From heaven I heard a voice, like the roar of many waters and like the sound of loud thunder; the voice I heard, like the sound of harpists playing on their harps. They sang a new song before the throne, and before the four living creatures and the elders; no one except the one hundred forty-four thousand who had been purchased from the earth could learn the song. These are the ones who have not made themselves unclean in relations with women for they have kept themselves celibate. It is these who follow the Lamb wherever he goes. They have been purchased from among humankind as first fruits to God and the Lamb. And in their mouth, no lie has been found for they are blameless.

1–5

The war of the worlds is occurring on earth between God and the evil threesome. John's fourth insight alludes to Psalm 2:6, the scripture behind the Lamb standing on Mt. Zion. Act IV depicts the nations and kings of the earth at war with the Lord and his anointed (Psalm 2:2), as seen in scenes one to three. In scene four, God installs his Messiah, the Lamb, on Mt. Zion with the 144,000, the Lamb's army seen in act II (7:4–8). The voice, like many waters, is like the wings of living beings (Ezekiel 1:24), Jesus's voice (1:15), and the voice of the great multitude (19:6). The twenty-four elders (5:9) sing a new song, praising the Lamb who alone is worthy. The 144,000 learn the new song, and all creation sings of the victory of Lamb (Psalm 96, 98; Isaiah 55:12–13).

Unfaithfulness to God (idolatry) is compared to adultery. The faithful 144,000, the bride of the Lamb, are undefiled by the corrupting influences of the unholy trinity. As an army, they symbolically abstain from sexual relations (Exodus 19:15; 1 Samuel 21:4–5). They follow the Lamb wherever he goes (Mark 8:34). The Lamb died for them. They belong only to him as an offering to God (Exodus 23:19). They are the first (fruits) of all who will come after them. In a contrast between truth and lies, the 144,000 are blameless (Zephaniah 3:13), faithful and true to the Lamb, while the dragon is the father of lies (John 8:44).

Scene Five: Three Angels, Two Choices (14:6–13)

Then I saw another angel flying in midheaven, having an eternal gospel to proclaim to those who dwell on earth, to every nation and tribe and tongue and people. And he said with a loud voice, "Fear God, and give him glory, because the hour of his judgment has come; worship him who made the heaven and the earth and the sea and the springs of waters."

And another angel, a second one, followed, saying, "Fallen, fallen is Babylon the great, who made all the nations drink of the wine of the passion of her immorality."

Then another angel, a third one, followed them, saying with a loud voice, "If anyone worships the beast and its image, and receives a mark on his forehead or on his hand, he also will drink of the wine of the wrath of God, mixed full strength into the cup of his anger; and he will be tormented with fire and brimstone in the presence of the holy angels and in the presence of the Lamb. And the smoke of their torment goes up forever and ever, and they have no rest day and night, these who worship the beast and its image, and whoever receives the mark of its name."

Here is the perseverance of the saints who keep the commandments of God and their faith in Jesus. And I heard a voice from heaven saying, "Write, 'Blessed are the dead who die in the Lord from now on!'" "Yes," says the Spirit, "so that they may rest from their labors, for their deeds follow them."

6–8

Scenes one to four follow the message of Psalm 2. John's fifth insight resembles the message of Psalm 1. Two choices, two ways: the righteous way of those who follow the Lamb and the wicked way of those who follow the beast. The first of three angels flying in midheaven, is seen, and heard by all, and proclaims the good news of the Lamb, announcing judgment is coming. There is time yet to worship the God who created all things (Genesis 1–2). Time remains to choose rightly. The second angel announces Babylon has fallen. This is language from prior judgments (Isaiah 21:9; Jeremiah 51:7–8). This is the first mention of Babylon in Revelation and a preview of the fate of the wicked coming in act VI.

9–13

The third angel describes in some detail the fate of those who worship the beast. John uses biblical imagery, the cup of God's wrath (Psalm 75:8; Isaiah 51:17), fire and brimstone, and smoke (Genesis 19:24–28) going up forever and ever (Isaiah 34:8–10). The imagery of torment forever and ever is examined more later. As a God of justice, God's anger is stirred over injustice. The martyrs cry out for justice (6:10), and a day of reckoning is coming (6:12–17). Justice must be served!

John's warning is to Christians, and it appears those who would be tormented are believers, those who let their guard down and expressed allegiance to the beast (Roman emperor) in order to escape suffering or even death. John must warn against going over to the dark side and leaving other believers at a greater risk. He pictures a fate worse than death, forsaking the truth (the Lamb) for a lie (the beast). This awful reality is pictured in horrific language of ever-lasting torment, symbolic yet real in its intent to persuade believers to remain faithful to the Lamb.

The alternative is also dreadful, if more and more forsake the Lamb to worship the beast. The church risks losing its witness to truth and reason for being. The fire may be God's chastising love, but it brings guilt worse than death for those who forsake the Lamb. It may seem the beast conquers the martyrs, but in truth, the martyrs conquer the beast by being faithful to the Lamb. The choice is clear: Persevere and keep the faith, no matter the cost. Blessed are the saints who from their labor rest.

Scene Six: The Harvest (14:14–20)

Then I looked, and saw a white cloud, and sitting on the cloud was one like a son of man, having a golden crown on his head and a sharp sickle in his hand. And another angel came out of the temple, crying out with a loud voice to the one who sat on the cloud, "Put in your sickle and reap, for the hour has come to reap, because the harvest of the earth is ripe." Then the one seated on the cloud swung his sickle over the earth, and the earth was reaped.

Then another angel came out of the temple in heaven, and he also had a sharp sickle. And another angel, the angel who has authority over fire, came out from the altar; and he called with a loud voice to the one who had the sharp sickle, saying, "Put in your sharp sickle and gather the clusters from the vine of the earth, because its grapes are ripe." And the angel swung his sickle over the earth and gathered the clusters from the vine of the earth, and threw them into the great wine press of the wrath of God. And the winepress was trodden outside the city, and blood flowed out from the wine press, up to the horses' bridles, for one thousand six hundred stadia (one hundred eighty miles).

14–16

John is granted this sixth insight into the cosmic battle between good and evil. This insight reveals the results of those choices made in scene five. The scene opens with one like a son of man. This is Jesus (1:13). Clouds are symbols of God's presence (Mark 9:7). Jesus wears the crown of the King of Kings. The sickle is a symbol of grain ready for the harvest (Mark 4:29). This scene contains two harvest images: the grain harvest (14–16) and the grape harvest (17–20).[15] Grain is not mentioned, but the first scene is clearly separate from the second scene of the grape harvest. The New Testament Greek word, *reap*, consistently refers to sowing and reaping. It means to harvest a crop where seed is broadcast (scattered) on the ground (John 4:36–38; 2 Corinthians 9:6). Reaping grain is usually a positive image in scripture (Romans 1:13).

This symbol of reaping applies to the ones who have been purchased as the first fruits (14:4; 1 Corinthians 15:23). They are the blessed ones who chose to follow the Lamb, even if need be to death (14:7, 12–13). There is also a dramatic difference between the two harvest scenes. Jesus only harvests the grain, the good harvest.

17–20

This second harvest scene begins with still another angel coming out of the temple, indicating, like the first scene, God is the Lord of the harvest. But this is a gathering of the grape harvest, the harvest of evil, and it is not Jesus, but an angel swinging a sharp sickle. Those who made the wrong choice to worship the beast are gathered like grapes, not reaped like grain. Fire is an image of judgment (8:5). Grapes and wine are symbols of God's wrath (14:8-11), as is the image of pressing grapes in the winepress (Isaiah 63:1–6). Such a vast amount of blood seems incomprehensible, flowing up to the horses' bridles for 1,600 stadia. The symbolism is of blood flowing over the earth. The number four stands for the earth. 4 x 4 = 16 *x* 10 (a round number) *x* 10 x 10 = 1,600.

Stadia is a Greek measurement of 600 feet, the length of a stadium. This scene of horror takes place outside the city. Jesus also was crucified outside the city gates (Hebrews 13:11–14). In a subtle way, this is a hint that the blood of Jesus can redeem even this vast river of blood. What can take away our sin? Nothing but the blood of Jesus! Amazing grace, it's sweet indeed, grace to meet our greatest need! Worthy is the Lamb that was slain!

Scene Seven: The Saints on the Glassy Sea (15:1–4)

Then I saw another sign in heaven, great and marvelous, seven angels with seven plagues, which are the last, because in them the wrath of God is finished. And I saw something like a sea of glass mixed with fire, and those who had conquered the beast and its image and the number of its name, standing upon the sea of glass, holding harps of God. And they sang the song of Moses, the bond-servant of God, and the song of the Lamb, saying,

> "Great and marvelous are your works,
>   O Lord God the Almighty!
> Just and true are your ways,
>   O King of the nations!
> Who will not fear, O Lord,
>   and glorify your name?
> For you alone are holy;
> for all the nations will come
> and worship before you,
> for your righteous acts have been revealed."

1–4

John's seventh insight into the battle between good and evil becomes a great cause of celebration, but that's not until verse two. Verse one gives a preview of act V, the seven angels with seven plagues. These will be the last. Like the plagues that accompanied the seven trumpets, these also are modeled after the Egyptian plagues against Pharaoh. This scene is a preview of the age to come. The saints have stepped through the darkness on this side and into the glorious light on the other side of the transition between the ages. John sees something like a sea of glass, which looks to be the same sea of glass that is before the throne of God (4:6). The sea represents the abode of evil (13:1). It was the barrier to the children of Israel escaping from Pharaoh (Exodus 14:9). But the sea is rendered harmless, turned into glass, a safe refuge on which to stand. This suggests the Israelites passing through the Reed Sea, through fire and water (Psalm 66:12).

Those who are standing on the glassy sea have conquered the beast. They are the martyrs who valued truth above their own lives, who never accepted the lie the beast is worthy of worship. They hold harps for praise and worship (Psalm 33:2, 81:2). Harps awaken the dawn (Psalm 57:8) to celebrate the dawning of a new day (Exodus 14:27). Morning has broken; God has spoken. Saints are adoring, casting their crowns upon the glassy sea (4:10). The saints, in triumph, sing the song of Moses (Exodus 15) and the song of the Lamb, a condensed version of the song of Moses, with similarities to Psalm 66. Great and marvelous are your works (Psalm 66:3). All the nations will come and worship before you (Psalm 66:4).

This is a story to tell to the nations, a tale of long ago at early dawn. At the darkest moment, when all seemed lost, God made a way. God conquered Pharaoh! Centuries later, after all seemed lost on an awful Friday, a few women showed up on Sunday at early dawn. God had conquered death. God makes a way for the followers of the way, for a people who joyfully sing the song of Moses and the song of the

Lamb. God has conquered death. Christ is risen indeed. Jesus is Victor! This scene helps to reinforce the message that God has made a way through the witness of the martyrs, for all the nations to come and worship God (11:13, 15:4).

Return with us now to earlier in the drama of Revelation, where every nation is created to worship God (4:11), the beast is granted authority over all nations to deceive with his lies (13:7), and the nations ignore all pleas to repent (14:6). And to follow the beast, they are hellbent (14:8) and suffer this fate worse than death (14:11). All the rebel nations with the beast have cast their lot, and to the lake of fire they must go, though the end of the story this is not (15:4). And although by the beast they are deceived, the lake of fire, will they leave?

Does the lake of fire rule out all hope? That's a question to pursue. As nations that appear lost (14:11) later appear to be saved (15:4), does Revelation leave any room for all to be saved? Yes, it does.[16] Because a pattern of salvation is following on the heels of judgment.

As seen in act IV, salvation (15:2–4) comes after judgment (14:6–20). This occurs again in act VII, as salvation (21:10–27) follows judgment (20:7-15).[17] Is forever and ever always forever and ever? Can it possibly be there is more to see? (1 Corinthians 15:22; Colossians 1:20) More later in the drama.

The Creator of the universe is beyond our human understanding until God is revealed through events and the symbols that give the events meaning. As examples, Jesus is the Lion, the Lamb, the Good Shepherd, and the Bread of Life. These symbols are part of God's revelation and are interpreted and give a much fuller picture of Jesus. The beast and the lake of fire are among a host of symbols that are essential to telling the Revelation story. Continuing with an examination of the lake of fire, it is fitting to review 14:10–11 and similar Revelation texts. Fire and brimstone (sulfur) and smoke are echoes of Sodom (Genesis 19:24–28), and these have become symbols of divine punishment.

Yet it seems to appear even a punishment so severe does not remove all hope of restoration. For Sodom, seemingly a favorite symbol of God's judgment can later experience restoration (Ezekiel 16:53–56).[18] In act VII, this dialogue about the lake of fire continues for a while, as the symbol is paired with another, the great high wall of the holy city with its gates open wide.

ACT V

Stage Setting (15:5–8)

The Temple Filled with God's Glory

After these things I looked, and the temple of the tabernacle of testimony in heaven was opened. and the seven angels with the seven plagues came out of the temple, clothed in clean, bright linen, and girded across their chests with golden sashes. Then one of the four living creatures gave the seven angels seven golden bowls full of the wrath of God, who lives forever and ever. And the temple was filled with smoke from the glory of God and from his power; and no one was able to enter the temple until the seven plagues of the seven angels were finished.

5–6

For Act V, the stage curtain is raised on God's heavenly throne room. God's temple remains as the stage setting as the drama continues. The tabernacle is the tent of testimony (Numbers 17:7). It held the Ten Commandments, which became known as the tablets of testimony (Exodus 32:15; Deuteronomy 10:5). The angels come out from the temple wearing golden sashes that show they are serving as priests. The golden bowls earlier held the prayers of the saints (5:8). The same saints later called out for justice (6:10, 8:3). "How long?

ACT V

How long, O Lord?" (Habakkuk 1:2). The seven trumpet plagues come as a warning to evildoers in response to the cries of the saints.

7–8

Now at last those bowls hold God's wrath. God's fury is directed against the cruelty of human beings, which they inflict upon each other. God expresses righteous rage over how his followers are being abused because they refuse to worship the beast. It's time for retribution to be poured out in answer to the saints' prayers for justice (Romans 12:19).

The temple fills with the smoke of God's glory and power (Exodus 40:34–35; 1 Kings 8:10–11). The smoke is also a sign of God's judgment (9:2–3). The prayers of the saints have been received and are being embraced with God's great glory and power. All else comes to a screeching halt as God's glory fills the temple. God is committed to securing justice for his suffering people. Everything can wait. The time is now!

93

ACT V

The Seven Bowls (16:1–16:17)

Scene One: The Bowl of Sores (16:1–2)

Then I heard a loud voice from the temple, saying to the seven angels, "Go and pour out upon the earth the seven bowls of the wrath of God." So, the first went and poured out his bowl on the earth; and it became a foul and malignant sore on the people who had the mark of the beast and who worshipped its image.

1

The scenes in the drama do not follow in chronological order. The drama is more like a collage, a visual technique with different parts assembled to make a new artistic creation. The seals, trumpets, and bowls are occurring together like three rings of an apocalyptic circus.[19] Revelation inspires the creative imagination as a visual work of art and a dramatic presentation of the written word. As a drama with seven acts of seven scenes, Revelation has a midpoint: act IV, scene four (the Lamb on Mt. Zion, 14:1–5). With the Lamb in the center, acts III (8:3–11:18) and V (15:5–16:17) become bookends for act IV.

And acts III (trumpets) and V (bowls) are similar scenes, best understood as expanded versions of the day of reckoning portrayed in act II, scene six (6:12–17). The plagues of both act III and V thereafter appear as the answer to the prayers of the saints (6:9–11) for justice. And the plagues are a warning for evil doers of a day of reckoning between the sufferings of this age and the glory of the age to come (Romans 8:18). God's justice is real, but humans cannot presume to fully understand it. No one can point here or there and say with any certainty, "That's God's judgment on evil!"

2

These acts performing in this three-ring apocalyptic circus come from scripture, including Sodom and Gomorrah, Moses and Pharaoh, God on Mt. Sinai, and the locusts of Joel. These acts also include the contemporary fear of earthquakes and enemy invasions. All these are part of the drama appearing on the center stage and portraying the symbolic world of Revelation. Take two Bibles. Open one to the trumpets and the other to the bowls. Notice the similarities. With the first trumpet (8:7) and the first bowl (16:2), the earth is struck. The first bowl brings sores on those who worship the beast (Exodus 9:10). What awful irony, those who seek compromise with the beast will become the ones who participate in suffering with the beast. A warning of a beastly fate indeed.

Scene Two: Bowl of Bloody Seas (16:3)

And the second poured out his bowl into the sea, and it became like the blood of a corpse; and every living thing in the sea died.

3

It's predictable that the second bowl, poured out into the sea, follows the pattern set by the second trumpet (8:8–9). But the trumpet plague changes only a third of the sea to blood while the bowl results in a total bloodbath with the death of every living thing. This series of plagues continue to model those against Pharaoh (Exodus

7:14–25). Moses had to face Pharaoh and his magicians, and the church must confront the idolatry of the Roman emperor and his underlings. All this blood is symbolism. The reality is a holy God who must stand for the truth.

Scene Three: Bowl of Bloody Rivers (16:4–7)

Then the third poured out his bowl into the rivers and the springs of water; and they became blood. And I heard the angel of the waters saying,

> "Just are you, O Holy One, who are and who were,
> because you judged these things;
> for they poured out the blood of saints and prophets,
> and you have given them blood to drink. They deserve it."

And I heard the altar saying,

> "Yes, O Lord God Almighty,
> true and just are your judgements."

4–7

Like the third trumpet plague (8:10–11), the freshwater is ruined as the bowl of wrath turns rivers and streams to blood. It's blood for blood. This gory scene is a human parable. Our wars run many a river red; yet for more blood, we seem to be led. If God did not despise the death of the innocent, God would be neither good nor holy. God must stand for the truth; reject the lie that wrong is right, that bad is good. But God gives us free will, a fearful power to choose. God gave us the antidote for all this bloodshed, the precious blood of the Lamb. Jesus shows us the way, though hearts not easily are swayed. God, just and true, have mercy on us all. Lord, have mercy! Christ, have mercy! Lord, have mercy upon us until this madness ceases and you are Lord of all.

Scene Four: The Bowl of Fiery Heat (16:8–9)

The fourth poured out his bowl upon the sun, and it was permitted to scorch people with fire. They were scorched with the fierce heat; and they blasphemed the name of God who has the authority over these plagues.

8-9

The fourth bowl plague strikes the sun, as did also the fourth trumpet plague (8:12). Yet while the trumpet ushered in the darkness upon the land, the bowl pours out the scorching heat. Here is a contrast with the martyrs who find protection from the sun's heat (7:16). This is a reminder of those for whom the psalmist writes, the sun will not smite by day (Psalm 121:6). But no such protection is assured for these who are to suffer from the awful scorching heat. Any warning goes unheeded as they continue to willingly blaspheme God's name.

The Bowl of Darkness and Pain (16:10–11)

Then the fifth poured out his bowl upon the throne of the beast, and its kingdom became darkened; and they gnawed their tongues in anguish and they blasphemed the God of heaven because of their pain and their sores; and they did not repent of their deeds.

10–11

Following the same pattern already mentioned, there are similarities between the plagues associated with the fifth bowl and those with the fifth trumpet (9:1–11). The darkness (9:2) and pain (9:5, 10) came with the fifth trumpet, and the fifth bowl also brings darkness and pain. This torment falls on the throne of the beast. This is the first specific warning given to Rome, the seat of earthly power and authority. It's an early warning of the judgment against Babylon (Rome) that is to follow in act VI. Pain and darkness are also associated with two of the plagues against Pharaoh: the pain suffered by those with the boils (Exodus 9:8–12) and the plague of darkness (Exodus 10:21–29). The plagues against Rome continue to mirror the plagues against Egypt. In response to their pain, the people blaspheme the God of heaven (Daniel 2:44), the God of earth. But no sign of repentance is yet to be seen. There is no sign, not even one, and not even a glimmer of remorse!

Scene Six: The Bowl of Demonic Spirits (16:12–16)

The sixth poured out his bowl on the great river, the Euphrates; and its water was dried up, to make way for the kings from the east. Then I saw, coming out of the mouth of the dragon and out of the mouth of the beast and out of the mouth of the false prophet, three unclean spirits like frogs. For they are demonic spirits, performing signs, who go out to the kings of the whole world, to gather them together for the war of the great day of God the Almighty. ("Look, I am coming like a thief. Blessed is the one who stays awake and keeps his clothes on, so that he will not walk about naked and people will not see his shame.") And they gathered them to the place which in Hebrew is called Harmageddon.

12–14, 16

Like the sixth trumpet plague, the sixth bowl targets the Euphrates River, the border between the Roman and Parthian empires. The river gave Rome the extra time needed to prepare for a Parthian invasion. But a dried up-river, a fearful sight to behold, is an invitation to armies from the east to invade. This is the era of wild conspiracies theories like the Nero myth, that a crazed, despotic Nero, returned from the dead (or from hiding), was coming at the head of the Parthian armies to conquer and destroy Rome. The demonic frog-like spirits mimic one of the plagues against Pharaoh (Exodus 8:1–15). These kings represent the entire inhabited earth, kings from beyond the Parthian and Roman Empires. They are all aligned against the Lamb and his army of martyrs (14:1–5).

The word *Harmageddon*, found only here in the Bible, appears to be two Hebrew words combined into one: Har (mountain) and Megiddon (Megiddo), the mountain of Megiddo. There is no Mt. Megiddo. There is the ancient city of Megiddo in Northern Palestine near Mt. Carmel. And several famous battles occurred near there (Judges 4; 2 Kings 9:27; 23:29–30). It's all symbolic. The Egyptian plagues have become magnified warnings of God's judgment on Rome. Contemporary fears of invasion from Parthian hordes are heightened. Visions of previous battles on bloodstained territory are expanded to picture all evil forces gathered in one place for God's great victory.

This victory has already occurred at one place. It's on the cross, where God's judgment fell and evil, sin, and death are defeated! Between two thieves on the cross, God gains the victory.

15

This verse in parenthesis is discussed separately. It's a blessing on a faithful church. Keep alert all the time for the coming of the Lamb. Don't go to sleep without keeping your clothes on. To get dressed, there is no time, with all the lives on the line. Jesus tells a parable in Matthew 24:42–51, using the illustration of a thief, to be alert and ready for his coming (2 Thessalonians 5:2–4; 2 Peter 3:10). Jesus is coming in power, coming in love. See the Lamb of God! He is already present here and now! Jesus is with us, Jesus is for us, and Jesus is near us in the lives of those around us. Are we ready for his coming? For he is already here.

Scene Seven: The Finished Bowl (16:17)

Then the seventh angel poured out his bowl upon the air, and a loud voice came out of the temple, from the throne, saying. "It is done."

17

The seventh angel empties his bowl's contents upon the air. There is a loud voice, "It is done!" This echoes from another time and place. A broken, bloodstained figure hangs between heaven and earth. He gasps for air; his blood stains the earth. The golden bowl takes on the shape of a bitter cup (John 18:11; John 19:28–30), and the Son of God says, "It is finished!"

What is done? What is finished? God, saddened and enraged over the terrible cost of the world's sin, drinks down the cup of his own wrath, now turned in against himself. Therefore, God is in Christ, reconciling the world to himself (2 Corinthians 5:17–19). On the third day, Jesus arose as victor over the dark powers of sin, death, and devil. Jesus's death is about much more than getting humans to heaven (a temporary stay). Jesus Christ died and rose again to launch the kingdom of God with humans here on earth (1 Corinthians 15:20–29). "It is finished!" Jesus is victor. God's eternal reign has begun. "It is done."

As with the other six bowls, the seventh bowl resembles the seventh trumpet. See act III, scene Seven (11:15), "The kingdom of the world has become the kingdom of our Lord; and of his Christ; and he will reign forever and ever." And lo, I am with you always (Matthew 28:20). For the Lord God, the Almighty reigns! King of Kings and Lord of Lords!

ACT VI

Stage Setting (16:18–17:2)

Warning of Babylon's Demise

And lightning flashed, and voices sounded, and thunder rumbled, and then a great earthquake such as there had not been since people came to be on earth, so great and mighty was the earthquake. The great city was split into three parts, and the cities of the nations fell. And God remembered to give Babylon the great the cup of the wine of his fierce anger. And every island fled away, and the mountains were not found. And huge hailstones, about one hundred pounds each, came down from heaven on people; and they blasphemed God because of the plague of the hail, because its plague was extremely severe.

Then one of the seven angels who had the seven bowls came and spoke with me, saying, "Come here, I will show you the judgment of the great harlot who sits on many waters, with whom the kings of the earth committed acts of immorality, and those who dwell on the earth were made drunk with the wine of her immorality."

18–21

These verses transition the drama to act VI. The lightning, voices, and thunder originate from God's throne (4:5). The earthquake is added (8:5), and the hail is next (11:19). Now the awful severity of the earthquake and the hail are magnified! The repetition of this series ties each act back to God's heavenly throne room (4:1–11) and back to God's awesome presence on Mt. Sinai, as Moses prepares to journey up the mountain and receive the Ten Commandments (Exodus 19:16). There, the people are warned, "Do not go near the mountain."

The earthquakes and darkness recall another throne scene of God's awful presence on a dark Friday as a cross becomes a throne (Matthew 27:33–54). The scenes in heaven (4:1–5:14) first set the stage for act II. This stage setting of the heavenly throne room then continues to remain as the background for each additional act as the drama unfolds.

1–2

Then one of the seven angels, with the seven bowls, speaks, suggesting what follows somehow continues the bowl plagues. And the next scene he is going to reveal to those who are following the drama will be amazing, horrifying, and disgusting. Babylon, the great city, is served notice! God's judgment will have the day, and no way will this go away. The kings of the earth (16:14) represent the nations allied with Rome.

ACT VI

Seven Words of Justice for Babylon (17:3–19:3)

Scene One: The Woman of Mystery (17:3–7)

And he carried me away in the Spirit into a wilderness; and I saw a woman sitting on a scarlet beast, full of blasphemous names, and having seven heads and ten horns. The woman was clothed in purple and scarlet, and adorned with gold and precious stones and pearls, holding in her hand a gold cup full of abominations and of the unclean things of her immorality, and on her forehead was written, a name of mystery: "Babylon the great, the mother of harlots and of earth's abominations." And I saw the woman drunk with the blood of the saints, and with the blood of the witnesses of Jesus. When I saw her, I was truly astonished! And the angel said to me, "Why are you so amazed? I will tell you the mystery of the woman, and of the beast with seven heads and ten horns which carries her."

3–4

John is carried away in the Spirit (1:10, 4:2) The Spirit is the Holy Spirit, not John's spirit as in some translations. His visions are explained as the intervention of the Holy Spirit (in the Spirit).

Act VI opens with a woman of mystery, who later is identified as Rome. She is a woman of luxury yet rotten to the core. Roman citizens saw the empire regularly portrayed on its coins and in statues as the goddess, Roma, the ideal woman of Roman society.

But John shows Roma as a wealthy, wanton prostitute, not at all as the golden goddess who is worshiped in the cities of the seven churches. The scarlet beast is the beast from the sea (Roman Empire), identified by its seven heads and ten horns. This horrid beast remains full of brazen blasphemes (13:6).

5–7

In scripture, unfaithfulness to the true God continues to be compared to unfaithfulness in marriage. Turning from God to idols not only is idolatry but also immorality (Ezekiel 23). Babylon, as the empire of Rome, is dead drunk with the saints' blood. This killing of other human beings has an intoxicating effect. It is the perverted elation of a bloodthirsty nation. With more bloodshed to be added, it's a shocking picture of the violence expected to come upon the churches. And the empire was thought to be the world's most advanced culture. John does more than wonder at the sight. He is more than amazed. He is astonished at what he is seeing. No wonder a just God is angry!

Scene Two: Mystery Explained (17:8–18)

The beast that you saw was and is not and is about to come up from the abyss and go to destruction. And those who dwell on the earth, whose name has not been written in the book of life from the foundation of the world, will be amazed when they see the beast, that it was and is not and will come.

This calls for a mind having wisdom. The seven heads are seven mountains on which the woman sits, and they are seven kings; five have fallen, one is, the other has not yet come; and when he comes, he will remain for a little while. The beast which was and is not, is also an eighth and is one of the seven, and it goes to destruction. The ten horns which you saw are ten kings who have not yet received a kingdom, but they are to receive authority as kings with the beast for one hour. These have one purpose, and they give their power and authority to the beast. These will wage war against the Lamb, and the Lamb will overcome them, because he is Lord of lords and King of kings, and the ones with him are the called and chosen and faithful.

Then he said to me, "The waters which you saw where the harlot sits, are peoples and multitudes and nations and tongues. And the ten horns which you saw, they and the beast will hate the harlot and will make her desolate and naked and will eat her flesh and will burn her up with fire. For God has put it in their hearts to do his will by having a common purpose of giving their kingdom to the beast, until the words of God are fulfilled. The woman whom you saw is the great city, which reigns over the kings of the earth."

8–11

God was, is, and is to come; the beast was and is not. The beast is explained, and the woman is next. In comparison to God, the beast is a nonentity, prepared for destruction. The names are written from time's beginning, from the world's foundation. Along with matter and energy, God created time. God spoke creation, including time, into being at the big bang, 13.7 billion years ago. Before the big bang, time does not exist. God dwells in eternity, in another dimension beyond time, in the eternal present. Therefore, God sees all of time at once. From the world's foundation to today and to the end of time, God is Lord over all time. God is the great I AM; the beast is not. Revelation may depart here from symbolism. Rome is built on seven hills. And some interpreters see the kings as eight Roman emperors.

- Augustus: 27 BC–AD 14
- Tiberius: AD 14–37
- Caligula: AD 37–41
- Claudius: AD 41–54
- Nero: AD 54–68
- Vespasian: AD 69–79
- Titus: AD 79–81
- Domition: AD 81–96

This does omit the three who briefly ruled in the months of chaos following Nero's death. Five have fallen. The sixth is Vespasian, and the one who comes next will remain only a little while (Titus who reigned two years). The eighth (Domition) is one of the seven. Perhaps a reference to the myth of Nero returning from the dead, meaning Domition (the new Nero), rules with Nero's same cruelty toward Christians. This suggests Revelation is written during the last years of Vespasian's reign (AD 75–79). See the introduction for the dating of Revelation and endnote number 1.

12–18

The Lamb overcomes because he is the King of Kings and Lord of Lords (19:11). He is the king who has already conquered on the cross and through his resurrection. The ones who are with him, the called, the chosen, and faithful ones, never give in to the unholy trinity's lies. The woman (Rome) enjoys a wide sphere of influence, ruling many nations and peoples. The ten kings (horns) are rulers aligned with Rome. This is symbolism of evil turning on evil, of God allowing evil to self-destruct. Those who live by the sword die by the sword (Matthew 26:52).

Pictured are horrors pulled from the pages of scripture. She will be hated and made naked and desolate. These are warnings against Babylon (Ezekiel 23:26–29; Isaiah 47:2–3). They will devour her flesh. This is the actual fate of Jezebel, a most despicable woman (2 Kings 9:30–37). They will burn her with fire. This is a fate mandated for a priest's daughter who loses her way (Leviticus 21:9). Revelation continually uses scripture in this way. When at last the angel reveals the mystery of the woman, she is the great city (Rome). With this revelation, justice for Rome is drawing ever closer.

Scene Three: The Fall of Babylon (18:1–3)

After these things I saw another angel coming down from heaven, having great authority, and the earth was illuminated with his glory. And he cried out with a mighty voice, saying,

> "Fallen, fallen is Babylon the great!
> She has become a dwelling place of demons
> and a haunt of every unclean spirit,
> and a haunt of very unclean and hateful bird.
> For all the nations have drunk of the passion of her immorality,
> and the kings of the earth have committed
> acts of immorality with her,
> and the merchants of the earth have grown
> rich by the wealth of her sensuality.

1–3

This next scene moves closer toward justice for Babylon with an announcement of her fall. This angel has great authority, coming directly from the presence of God with the glory of God clinging to him like a mantle (Exodus 34:29–35). This glory illumines the earth (Ezekiel 43:2). With a mighty voice, the angel cries out his pronouncement on the fall of Babylon (Rome). The great city is fallen (Isaiah 21:9) and becomes a forsaken place, a dwelling for the demons and the birds. John's source for the demons appears to be those shaggy goats who are said to be demonic creatures and supposedly inhabit the desolate places apart from human society (Isaiah 13:20–22, 34:11–15).

This theme of drunkenness describes Rome's unrestrained indulgence (17:6). Rome is intoxicated with the sin of idolatry and immorality (Jeremiah 51:7). Because the kings and merchants of the earth have become wealthy through Rome's excesses, they participate gladly in her debauchery. The kings and merchants will appear later in more detail (18:9–20). This comes as a warning for the seven churches against joining the trade guilds in order to gain economic prosperity. To join the trade guilds means eating meat sacrificed to idols, and by doing this, they are in contact with emperor worship. One thing continues to lead to another and another and then at last to spiritual ruin.

Scene Four: The Sins of Babylon (18:4–8)

Then I heard another voice from heaven, saying,

> "Come out of her, my people,
> so that you will not share in her sins
> and of her plagues you will not receive.
> for her sins have piled up as high as heaven,
> and God has remembered her iniquities,
> Pay her back even as she has paid back,
> and give back to her double according to her deeds,
> and in the cup which she has mixed, mix twice as much for her.
> To the degree that she has glorified herself and lived sensuously,
> to the same degree give her torment and mourning,
> for she says in her heart,
> "I rule as a queen
> and I am not a widow,
> and mourning, I will never see."

Therefore, in one day her plagues will come,
pestilence and morning and famine,
and she will be burned up with fire,
for the Lord God who judges her is strong.

4–8

Another scene and another voice cry out for justice to Babylon, a voice from heaven from where two previous angels came to warn of coming doom. It's an urgent warning to come out of Babylon (Isaiah 52:11). This is a tale of two cities. Near the end of Revelation (22:14), believers are called to enter the city of New Jerusalem. But in order to enter New Jerusalem, Christians must first come out of Babylon. They must separate themselves from Rome's idolatry and immorality, as it was being lived out in their cities in Asia Minor. If not, her sins and plagues will taint her. The messages to the seven churches warn that believers are becoming entangled in her sins and trapped in her lies. Rome's sins are stacked high (Genesis 11:4); they are piled up to heaven (Jeremiah 51:9). Yet there is no thought of confession before God, who is higher still (Isaiah 55:8–9).

This call for revenge, to pay her back, is an echo from long ago. In Babylon, a Jewish exile writes of captivity in a foreign land. Feeling the anguish and anger, he cries out for vengeance, having been forced into exile when Babylon destroyed Jerusalem in 587 BC (Psalm 137). Revelation doesn't shy away from raw emotions, but what about paying her back double for her sins? The background of this verse comes from Israel's sins (Isaiah 40:2; Jeremiah 16:18). The meaning may not be to double punishment, but to match the intensity of the sin committed.

Believers are unable to pay back her sins, which goes against all Christian teaching. The ten kings turn on Babylon (17:12–16) and pay her back. "Vengeance is mine; I will repay" (Deuteronomy 32:35;

Romans 12:19). Human arrogance knows no bounds (Proverbs 29:23); pride goes before a fall (Proverbs 16:18). Such boasting is the height of arrogance, but soon the truth will be revealed. John draws on prophesies against the actual Babylon for these voices of doom against Rome. He echoes Isaiah's lament over Babylon centuries before Revelation (Isaiah 47:6–8; Psalm 10:6). And doom is sure (Jeremiah 50:31–32).

Scene Five: A Threefold Lament, The Kings' Lament (18:9–10)

And the kings of the earth, who committed acts of immorality and lived luxuriously with her, will weep and lament over her when they see the smoke of her burning. They stand at a distance because of the fear of her torment, saying,

> 'Woe, woe, the great city,
> Babylon, the mighty city!
> For in one hour your judgment has come."

9-10

This exact phrase, the kings of the earth, appears frequently in the Revelation drama (6:15, 17:2, 18, 18:3, 9, 19:19, 21:24), besides other references to kings. These kings seem to be the leaders of all the nations who participate with Rome in trade and finance. Seeing their golden goose cooked, burned to a blackened crisp, they add their voice of doom to prior voices. Engaging in trade, they supported the emperor worship of the trade guilds, indirectly adding to the suffering of believers who refused to participate in Rome's idolatry and immorality. Many people get too close to the fire. It's best to stay back or else get burnt. Fire often brought great destruction to ancient cities. Fire burned much of Rome in AD 64. Fire is a symbol of judgment. The hour of judgment has come. Similar judgments

ACT VI

are found in the lament against Tyre in Ezekiel 27. Half the items of commerce in Ezekiel's lament are found here also.

John echoes the example of ancient Tyre. Like Rome, Tyre was a thriving economic power of commerce and trade, wealthy, proud, and seemingly indestructible. This Phoenician city, south of modern Beirut, Lebanon, was really two cities, one on the coast and the other off the coast on an island. Soon after Ezekiel's lament, the mainland city was attacked by the Babylonians, under Nebuchadnezzar. Its inhabitants were resupplied through two harbors and held out thirteen years before Babylon destroyed the city.

But the island city remained untouched until Alexander the Great attacked both cities (333–332 BC). His armies destroyed the city on land and filled the sea with enough debris to reach the island. After a seven-month siege, the island city fell. If ancient Tyre fell, so can Rome. The lament of the kings is comparable to that of the merchants and mariners that follow, more laments of self-interest. And now on to the next scene.

Scene Five: A Threefold Lament, The Merchants' Lament (18:11–17a)

And the merchants of the earth weep and mourn over her, because no one buys their cargo anymore-cargoes of gold and silver and precious stones and pearls and fine linen and purple and silk and scarlet, and citron wood and every product of ivory, and every product from very costly wood, and bronze and iron and marble, and cinnamon and spices and incense and perfume and frankincense and wine and olive oil and fine flour and wheat and cattle and sheep, and cargoes of horses and chariots and slaves, that is human lives.

The fruit you desire
has gone from you,

and all things that were luxurious and splendid
are lost to you
and people will no longer find them.

The merchants of these wares, who became rich from her, will stand at a distance because of the fear of her torment, weeping and mourning, saying,

"Woe, woe, the great city,
she who was clothed in fine linen
and purple and scarlet,
and adorned with gold
and precious stones and pearls;
for in one hour such great wealth has been laid waste!"

11–17a

Mention of slaves draws a sharp contrast between the church and the empire. Bodies is the literal word used for slaves. Human lives were nothing but bodies to be used, broken, and destroyed by a wealthy class living in luxury. Some estimates place the number of slaves in the Roman empire as high as sixty million. Jesus is crystal clear about slavery, "The Spirit of the Lord is upon me ... he sent me to proclaim release to the captives ... to set free those who are oppressed ... (Luke 4:18). The lament of the merchants who became rich from Rome's trade are much like the laments of the kings of the earth. These laments echo the lamentation over Tyre in Ezekiel 27.

Scene Five: A Threefold Lament,
The Mariners' Lament (18:17b–20)

And every shipmaster and every seafarer and sailor, and as many as make their living by the sea, stood at a great distance, and were crying out as they saw the smoke of her burning, saying, "What city is like the great city?" And they threw dust on their heads and were crying out, weeping, and mourning, saying,

> "Woe, woe, the great city
> in which all who had ships at sea
> became rich by her wealth,
> for in one hour she has been laid waste!
> Rejoice over her, O heaven,
> and you saints and apostles and prophets,
> because God has determined justice for you against her."

17b–20

A great part of Rome's commerce was by ships; the shipmaster was the ship's pilot (the captain). Like the kings and merchants, the mariners watch helplessly in horror and disbelief as the great city burns. They mourn for the luxury of a lost way of life. "What city is like the great city?" (Ezekiel 37:32). The dust placed on the head is a sign of mourning (Job 2:12; 1 Samuel 4:12). God brings justice against Babylon for the martyrs who cried out for justice in act II.

Let's review. It begins with the martyrs' plea, "How long, O Lord?" (6:10) A day of reckoning, a day of judgment, is forecast in response to their plea (6:12–17). The prayers of the saints, for vengeance and justice, are mixed with incense and thrown to earth (8:3–5). The seven trumpets of judgment follow (8:7–9:21). The faithful witness of the martyrs leads the nations to repentance and faith (11:13). The evil powers behind the suffering of the martyrs, the unholy trinity, are introduced (12:1–13:18). More scenes of justice and reward follow (14:1–20). The sequence of the seven trumpets (8:6–11:16) is repeated by the seven angels with the seven bowls (5:8, 16:1–17). The scenes of judgment, specifically on Rome, are repeated in the seven words of justice for Babylon.

At last, the martyrs can rejoice. Their pleas for justice are answered (18:20). Revelation may be understood as a commentary on Romans 12:19–21. The saints and martyrs do not seek their own revenge, but leave it to the wrath of God. They overcome by the word of God and the testimony of Jesus Christ.

Scene Six: Babylon's Violent End (18:21–24)

Then a mighty angel took up a stone like a great millstone and threw it into the sea, saying,

> "So, will be thrown down with violence,
> Babylon, the great city
> and will not be found any longer;
> and the sound of harpists and musicians
> and flute players and trumpeters
> will not be heard in you any longer;
> and all craftsman of any craft
> will not be found in you any longer;
> and the sound of a mill
> will not be heard in you any longer;
> and the light of a lamp
> will not shine in you any longer;
> and the voice of the bridegroom and bride
> will not be heard in you any longer;
> for your merchants were the elite of the earth,
> because all the nations were deceived by your sorcery.
> And in her was found the blood of prophets and of saints
> and of all who have been slain on the earth."

21–24

The symbolism is from Jeremiah, who wrote of calamity to fall on ancient Babylon when the Persians invaded in 539 BC. The city was destroyed, never again to reach its former splendor. He wrote in a scroll and gave instructions it should be read to Hebrew exiles in Babylon and thrown into the Euphrates with a stone attached (Jeremiah 51:59–64). This third mighty angel brings a conclusion to the events initiated by the first two angels (5:2, 10:1) and spelled out in detail in acts II through VI. The kings, merchants, and mariners look upon Babylon's demise from a distance. This is a sad and tragic scene of a city when all aspects of daily life come to a screeching halt. John draws on other images of cities in ruin (Isaiah 23:8, 24:8; Jeremiah 7:34).

Revelation is packed with violent images of a violent world. Blood runs red, and martyrs plead for justice (6:9–11). God answers with the seven trumpets, the seven bowls, and finally the seven words of justice for Babylon. The vision of the light going out is particularly tragic, yet a grace-filled reminder of the Light the darkness cannot put out (John 1:5). The merchants who thought themselves special are blinded by the wealth and privilege won on the backs of the poor ground into the dust. No nation can become great until the worth of all its citizens is recognized, and Rome failed miserably.

Throughout Revelation, the blood of the martyrs continues the plea to God begun by the blood of Abel (Genesis 4:10). As act VI of the grand drama draws to a close, God continues to call for faithful witnesses to the truth, with reminders along the way that God prefers not to destroy but for evildoers to change their ways. And judgment is held back again and again and again. These horrors are symbolic, but God's judgment is real. How long is the patience of a just God? Is there yet time for mercy?

Scene Seven: The Lord's Vengeance (19:1–6)

After these things I heard something like a loud voice of a great multitude in heaven, saying,

"Hallelujah!
Salvation and glory and power belong to our God.
for his judgments are true and just;
for he has judged the great harlot
who was corrupting the earth with her immorality,
and he has avenged on her,
the blood of his bond-servants."

And a second time they said,

"Hallelujah!
Her smoke rises up forever and ever."

And the twenty-four elders and the four living creatures fell and worshiped God who sits on the throne saying,

"Amen. Hallelujah!"

And a voice came from the throne, saying,

"Give praise to out God,
all you his bond-servants,
you who fear him,
the small and the great."

And I heard something like the voice of a great multitude and like the voice of many waters and like the voice of mighty peals of thunder, saying,

"Hallelujah!
For the Lord our God,
the Almighty, reigns."

1–6

A seventh scene opens with hallelujahs of the worshiping heavenly multitude. God has answered the martyrs' pleas for vengeance on Rome (6:10). God has judged, found the empire guilty, and rendered justice (Deuteronomy 32:35; Romans 12:19). The heavenly multitude sings again the Salvation Hymn (7:9–10, 12:10), a direct challenge to the Roman emperor who claims to be the empire's only savior. With the fourfold hallelujah, the original Hallelujah Chorus, the heavenly multitude celebrates God's victory, joined in ceaseless praise by the twenty-four elders and the four living creatures (Psalm 19:9; Isaiah 34:10). Singing joyful hymns of praise and hallelujahs, the heavenly choir closes act VI with a standing ovation that brings down the house. As the curtain falls, the drama cannot yet be over. Prepare now to experience the climatic act VII of the Revelation drama.

ACT VII

Stage Setting (19:7–10)

The Marriage Supper of the Lamb

> "Let us rejoice and be glad
> and give God the glory,
> for the marriage of the Lamb has come
> and his bride has made herself ready.
> It was given to her to clothe herself in fine linen,
> bright and clean;
> for the fine linen is the righteous deeds of the saints."

And he said to me, "Write, 'Blessed are those who are invited to the marriage supper of the Lamb.'" And he said to me. "These are true words of God." Then I fell at his feet to worship him. But he said to me, "Do not do that; I am a fellow servant with you and your brothers and sisters who hold the testimony of Jesus; worship God." For the testimony of Jesus is the spirit of prophesy.

7–10

This ecstatic celebration of the empire's demise included the Hallelujah Chorus and the Salvation Hymn. These now blend into the marvelous Marriage Song of the Lamb (Isaiah 61:10). God's marriage to his people is a theme throughout the prophets and the New Testament. Israel is God's unfaithful wife (Hosea 2). The faithful city becomes faithless (Isaiah 1:21). Jerusalem's unfaithfulness continues (Jeremiah 2:20). In exile, Israel returns as God's bride (Isaiah 54:4–7). Jerusalem has been claimed by God to be his bride, yet again becomes unfaithful (Ezekiel 16:8–14).

In the New Testament, Paul compares the church as a bride presented to Christ, her husband (2 Corinthians 11:2). In another example from Paul, the marriage of husband and wife is compared to the mystery of the church as the bride of Christ (Ephesians 5:32). In Revelation, the martyred church, clothed in her wedding garments, is ready to meet her husband, the Lamb. Next the bride, clothed in her same fine linen, becomes the Lamb's army, accompanying him as he comes from heaven to earth (19:14). The marriage supper of the Lamb is made ready. Blessed are those who are invited to attend. The marriage of the Lamb and his church is symbolic of heaven and earth coming together. The two parts of God's good creation are reunited as intended from the beginning.[20]

ACT VII

Seven Visions of Christ's Return (19:11–22:5)

Scene One: The One True King of Kings (19:11–16)

And I saw heaven opened, and look, a white horse, and he who sat on it is called Faithful and True, and in righteousness he judges and makes war. His eyes are a flame of fire, and on his head are many diadems; and he has a name written on him which no one knows except himself. He is clothed with a robe dipped in blood, and his name is called the Word of God. And the armies which are in heaven, clothed in fine linen, white and clean, were following him on white horses. From out of his mouth comes a sharp sword, so that he will strike down the nations, and he will shepherd them with a rod of iron; and he treads the winepress of the furious anger of God, the Almighty. And on his robe and where his garment covers his thigh, he has a name written, "King of Kings, and Lord of Lords."

11–12

At last, the great drama's seventh and last act has begun. Who comes riding a white horse? Zorro? The Lone Ranger? No! It's the Lamb astride a prancing, white stallion, the mount of generals and kings!

The earlier white horse and its rider (6:1–2) are but a parody of the true King of Kings. Seven attributes of the lamb are listed (verses 11–13), with four more to follow later (verses 15–16).[21]

Faithfulness is the essence of the Lamb's identity, and truthfulness is the sum of his testimony (3:14, 21:5, 22:6; Psalm 96:13). His word is truth (John 17:17). In righteousness, he judges the poor justly (Isaiah 11:4; Psalm 89:14), fighting fiercely against every lie and falsehood. No lie endures his flaming, piercing eyes (1:14; Daniel 12:6). Acting in justice and equality (Psalm 72:2, 98:9), with jeweled crowns (royal diadems), awesome power he is displaying (Isaiah 62:3); with a name only the Father knows, a name of mystery he is bearing. In ancient society, to know a name meant gaining control over a person. The unknown name, like the name I AM revealed to Moses (Exodus 3:13–14), is revealed only at God's discretion (Matthew 11:27). When he comes, we shall know him as he is (1 John 3:1–2).

13–16

His robe is covered with (dipped in) blood. Whose blood is this? There is no agreement on the source of the blood. Is it Christ's own blood shed upon the cross? Is it the blood of the martyrs whom Christ holds in his loving embrace? Is it the blood of his enemies from the symbolism of the winepress (14:20)? The blood's source may not be known, but the view here is that it is the Lamb's own blood. And a known name, the word of God, the Lamb is now bearing (Isaiah 40:8).

In act II, the fiery red, black, and pale horse (6:3-8) follow the white horse as sword, famine, and death. Not so for the true and faithful Lamb on the white horse, as his army of martyrs follow him, not in death, but in resurrected life. He leads an army riding on white horses, his bride, clothed in wedding garments (19:8). The Lamb strikes the nations with the sharp sword from his mouth (19:21,

Isaiah 49:2). This keen sword is the word of God (Hebrews 4:12). He is fully armed with the word of truth (John 17:17), the truth to conquer the devil's lies. The battle is all about competing testimonies and lordships. Is Jesus Lord, or is Caesar lord?[22]

The martyrs' testimony drew first blood and brought down the armies of the beast (12:11). Jesus leads with a shepherd's rod (Psalm 2:9) and treads the winepress of God's furious anger (Isaiah 63:3). Why is God so angry? Because he loves us (1:5). God is love (1 John 4:8). God's great love lashes out in fury over humans killing one another.

Yes, the blood on Jesus's robe is the Lamb's own blood. It's God's blood (2 Corinthians 5:19), shed out of love for the world, outside the gates of the city (Mark 15:22–24). Jesus is King of Kings, Lord of Lords. He is exercising authority over the nations through his victorious death on the cross. Jesus is Victor! Hallelujah! Hallelujah! All evil powers the Lamb has overcome (Colossians 1:13–20).

All descriptions of Jesus make this one point: he who comes has already come and has fundamentally changed the world and overcome all opposition to his reign, and he's already known in the faith of his church, as the redeemer, revealer, and Lord. He's about to step from the heavenly shadows into the radiant light of his unveiled existence to vindicate his church's faith.[23] Shall the darkness overcome him? Never. For he shall reign forever and ever, which is truly forever. All praises to our God and King! Throughout the heavens, his praises ring!

Scene Two: The Great Supper of Doom (19:17–21)

Then I saw an angel standing in the sun, and he cried out with a loud voice to all the birds which fly in mid-heaven, "Come, gather for the great supper of God, so that you may eat the flesh of kings and the flesh of commanders and the flesh of mighty men and the flesh of horses and of those who sit on them and the flesh of all, both free and slaves, and small and great."

Then I saw the best and the kings of the earth and their armies assembled to make war against him who sat on the horse and against his army. And the best was seized, and with it the false prophet who performed the signs in its presence, by which it deceived those who had received the mark of the beast and those who worshiped its image; these two were thrown alive into the lake of fire which burns with brimstone. And the rest were slain with the sword which came out from the mouth of him who sat on the horse, and all the birds were filled with their flesh.

17–21

This scene appears to picture the carnage of a great battle occurring between verses 16 and 17. The great supper of God is a parody of the marriage supper of the Lamb, the true reality (19:7–10). John's source appears to be Ezekiel 38–39. The birds fly in mid-heaven where all may hear their invitation to the feast (Ezekiel 39:17–20). This scene finally completes the day of reckoning in act II, scene six (6:12–17). A similar cast of characters appears here from act II: the kings and generals and the free and the slave. The battle is no contest for the rider on the white horse who won the great victory through his own death and resurrection (John 19:30).

The beast from the sea is seized; the bow of this fake rider on a white horse is powerless to save him (6:1–2). Taken with him is the false prophet. With the demise of the symbolic figures of the beast from the sea and the false prophet (the beast from the land), John portrays a fiery end of the idolatry of emperor worship. This horrid torture scene of everlasting torment is meant to scare believers into going straight, a gruesome site meant to transform present behavior.

Others are killed by the sword of God's eternal word (Hebrews 4:12–13), meaning that truth prevails and deception fails. God's word overcomes the forces of evil. All flesh is as grass, but God's word forever lasts (Isaiah 40:6–8).

Scene Three: The Millennial Kingdom, Reign of the Saints (20:1–6)

Then I saw an angel coming down from heaven, holding in his hand the key of the abyss and a great chain. And he seized the dragon, the serpent of old, who is the devil and Satan, and bound him for a thousand years; and he threw him into the abyss, and shut it and sealed it over him, so that he would not deceive the nations any longer, until the thousand years were completed; after these things he must be released for a short time.

Then I saw thrones, and judgment was given to they who sat on them, And I saw the souls of those who had been beheaded because of their testimony of Jesus and because of the word of God; and those who had not worshiped the beast or its image, and had not received the mark on their forehead and on their hand. They came to life and reigned with Christ for a thousand years. The rest of the dead did not come to life until the thousand years were completed. This is the first resurrection. Blessed and holy is the one who has a part in the first resurrection; over these the second death has no power, but they will be priests of God and of Christ and will reign with him for a thousand years.

1–3

Bible students know the thousand years as the millennium. About the binding of Satan, Jesus had already spoken (Mark 3:27). Satan's defeat is earlier reported (12:7–9). It's a defeat secured on the cross (Luke 10:18). With the Lamb's return, the light of truth exposes

Satan's lies. With his defeat complete, he is imprisoned in the realm of the dead: Sheol (Hebrew) or Hades (Greek), known as a prison (1 Peter 3:18–20). The Lamb is victorious, and Satan is defeated. Truth wins, and lies lose. Entire theological doctrines are built around the millennium, which appears nowhere in scripture except in Revelation 20. This is a very brief summary of the principle doctrines:

1. Post-millennialism teaches that the preaching of the gospel will continue to bring about a better world until the millennium comes, followed by Christ's return after the millennium.[24]
2. Pre-millennialism teaches the world will get worse until Christ returns before the millennium begins.
3. Pre-millennial dispensationalism is a variation of number two. It teaches that the world will get so bad that Christ will come and rapture the church out of the world so believers may be saved from seven years of terrible world suffering, and then Christ will come yet another time to bring in the millennium.[25]
4. Amillennialism teaches the thousand years is symbolic. Often in this doctrine, the millennium refers to the church age, from Pentecost to Christ's return, which is expected after the symbolic millennium is complete.[26]

None of these doctrines, including number four, are adequate to explain the thousand years. In the interpretation to be given here, the millennium is symbolic but quite different from number four.

4–6

Satan is imprisoned. Now what? The thrones are an important clue. With Satan locked up, the souls of the martyrs are called to render judgment (Daniel 7:9). These same souls first appear under the altar in act II, scene five, the fifth seal (6:9–11). The beast from the sea had been granted authority over these saints for forty-two months (13:5) in order to overcome them (13:7). These saints are the triumphant church (7:9–17). Also, among them are those who had not worshipped the beast but had escaped martyrdom. They are the militant church (7:4–8). In the view from earth, the beast overcomes the martyrs.

But heaven's view is what counts. The martyrs render judgment on the beast and its insidious instigator, Satan. The martyrs overcome by the blood of the Lamb and the word of their testimony (12:11). The unholy trinity is destroyed (19:20, 20:10), and the kingdom is transferred to the saints (20:4–6), as depicted in Daniel (7:18). The destroyer is destroyed, and the martyrs are rewarded (11:18). The millennium is a symbolic number, which is meant to show heaven's view of the martyrs' triumph. The beast rules for only forty-two months (13:5), but the martyrs reign for a thousand years!

To emphasize this again: The millennium is a symbolic number used to draw a contrast between the martyrs' reign and the beast's reign. Forty-two months is nothing compared to a thousand years, and even a thousand years is nothing in God's sight (Psalm 90:4). In this corner, the saints' thousand-year reign! And in that corner is the beast's forty-two-month conquest of the saints. There is no contest. The martyrs win! The evil threesome loses![27]

Scene Three Continued: The Release of Satan (20:7–10)

When the thousand years are completed, Satan will be released from his prison, and he will come out to deceive the nations which are in the four corners of the earth, Gog, and Magog, to gather them together for the war; the number of them is like the sand of the seashore. And they came up on the broad plain of the earth and surrounded the camp of the saints and the beloved city, and fire came down from heaven and devoured them. And the devil who deceived them was thrown into the lake of fire and brimstone, where the beast and the false prophet are also; and they will be tormented day and night forever and ever.

7–10

The release of Satan is among the most difficult and strangest verses to wrap our minds around. Why allow Satan a get-out-of-jail-free card? After his release, he gathers the nations from the earth's four corners to war against the saints. These same saints are the armies of resurrected martyrs who accompanied the Lamb (19:14), the same martyrs who had overcome the beast and reign symbolically for a thousand years. Who are these nations from the earth's four corners who come together to form Satan's sadistic army? What is this great battle? A possible interpretation is that this is a retelling of the Lamb's victory, which earlier is identified as the great supper of God (19:17–21). If so, the results are quite predictable, with the same defeat as shown the first time.

Another possible interpretation of Satan's army is that it's made up of demonic forces from the underworld, hordes from the ends of the earth. This is a legion of fiends recruited from the cellars of Hades. These innumerable shadowy forces of death, Gog, and Magog (Ezekiel 38–39), rise to attack the resurrected saints. But death stands no chance to conquer resurrected life. These hordes of demons from the pit are soon burnt to a crisp and disappear in a puff of smoke.[28] O death, where is your victory? (1 Corinthians 15:55).

The forces of death can never reverse the triumph of Christ's great kingdom of love and light. Satan runs out of hiding places. There is nowhere else to go but the lake of fire. The saints continue to reign. Christ's kingdom is forever! God wins! Satan loses!

Scene Four: Judgment Day (20:11–15)

Then I saw a great white throne and him who sat upon it, from whose presence earth and heaven fled, but no place was found for them. And I saw the dead, the great and the small, standing before the throne, and books were opened; and another book was opened, which is the book of life; and the dead were judged from the things which were recorded in the books, according to their works. And the sea gave up its dead which were in it, and death and hades gave up the dead which were in them; and they were judged, every one of them according to their works. Then death and hades were thrown into the lake of fire. This is the second death, the lake of fire. And if anyone's name was not found recorded in the book of life, he was thrown into the lake of fire.

11–13

It's judgment day! Heaven and earth flee away. The old heaven and earth are gone, and the new is coming right along (21:1). As Jesus's return (19:11–16) ushers in these next scenes, this is more like a collage with no clear sequence of events. The saints who are reigning for a thousand years (20:4–6) are among these resurrected dead, the great and the small, who belong to Christ at his coming (1 Corinthians 15:23). The books are opened (Daniel 7:10), the Books of Works and Book of Life.

In the parable of the last judgment (Matthew 25:31–46), it seems those caring for the needy didn't even know they had ministered to Jesus. They are motivated by compassion (Ephesians 2:8–10). And what of those, whose names may be missing in the Book of Life? Are they too prideful in their own works in their own confession (Matthew 7:21–23)? It's all by grace as we run this race. Only the Lamb is worthy!

14–15

The second death is the lake of fire. The beast and false prophet are these symbolic figures cast into the fire to show the demise of pride and arrogance epitomized by Rome. It looks like the death of evil, but not yet. Satan still hangs around since he was taken from underground. And in some way, Satan becomes a symbolic way of expressing the magnitude and gravity of the terrible evil that we are unable to grasp with heart or mind. What does it mean that this embodiment of evil is tormented forever (20:10)? And are others consigned to eternal torment without hope? Or is the fire God's chastising love (14:11, 15:4)?

A first resurrection (20:5–6) suggests a second resurrection. It will not do to interpret a second resurrection as being for unbelievers to be cast into the fire. Resurrection does not bring death but instead redemption and life. As the first resurrection brings redemption from the first death, it would seem to follow that a second resurrection brings redemption from the second death.[29] And then what follows is the blessed hope of reconciliation for all humanity, even the universe (Romans 8:19–22). Dare we believe our God is big enough? Look at this from another scripture, "In Christ all shall be made alive" (1 Corinthians 15:22). Christ is resurrected. Then those who are Christ's at his coming are resurrected. Then comes the end, a third event, the resurrection of all (1 Corinthians 15:20–28)?

Universal salvation seems not beyond the realm of possibility. The purpose here is to raise that possibility because with God all things are possible (Matthew 19:26). God is more amazing than can be imagined, and we see now only with the dimmest of eyes (1 Corinthians 13:12). Hold your horses. This will still be examined later.

Scene Five: The New Heaven and New Earth (21:1–8)

Then I saw a new heaven and a new earth; for the first heaven and the first earth passed away, and there is no longer any sea. And I saw the holy city, new Jerusalem, coming down out of heaven from God, made ready as a bride adorned for her husband. And I heard a loud voice from the throne, saying,

> "Look, the tabernacle of God is among people,
>   and he will dwell among them,
>   and they shall be his people,
>   and God himself will be among them.
> And he will wipe away every tear from their eyes,
>   and there will no longer be any death;
> there will no longer be any mourning, or crying, or pain,
>   for the former things have passed away."

And he who sits on the throne said, "Look, I am making all things new." And he said, "Write, for these words are faithful and true." Then he said to me, "It is done! I am the Alpha and the Omega, the beginning, and the end. I will give to the thirsty from the spring of the water of life without cost. Those who overcome will inherit these things, and I will be their God and they will be my children. But for the cowardly and unbelieving and abominable and murderers and immoral persons and sorcerers and idolaters and all liars, their portion will be in the lake that burns with fire and brimstone, which is the second death."

1–4

God enters the scene; the old heaven and earth flee away (20:11). The new is coming (Isaiah 65:17, 66:22), a transformation of the old into the new. There is no more sea, symbolic for evil and defiance to God. The beast's abode is gone (13:1). There's no room for evil in

God's new home, as heaven and earth come together as one. New Jerusalem is coming (21:9–27). From the throne, a voice is calling. God's tabernacle among people is coming. Even as God dwelt in an earthly tabernacle, his glory brought heaven and earth together (Exodus 40:34–38; Leviticus 26:11), if only for the briefest hour.

Among us, Jesus comes to dwell, the old story we love to tell. But Revelation has no rapture of believers to heaven. The city of God is coming to earth. Believers are meant for an earth transformed.[30] To God's good earth, salvation is coming; salvation coming to birds and bees, flowers, and trees, all for God's good pleasure (Colossians 1:19–20). God comes among us to dwell. No more dying; no more crying! Death is swallowed up! Tears are wiped away (Isaiah 25:8)! Death, the last enemy, is defeated! Abolished (1 Corinthians 15:26)!

5–7

God speaks for only the second time in Revelation. Listen! Listen! God confirms the truth: all things are made new. God is faithful and true (Deuteronomy 7:9, 2 Timothy 2:13). It's done. Finished (15:1, 17:17)! This is an echo of another time and place as the Son of God hung on a Roman cross, his work done. The battles in Revelation are mop-up actions of last-ditch efforts from a vanquished foe. As stated, God speaks only for the second time, "It is done!" The Lamb had already won God's decisive battle on a dark Friday as he cried out, "It is finished!" (John 19:30). God says, "I am the Alpha and the Omega" (1:8, 21:6). Christ replies, "I am the Alpha and the Omega (1:17, 22:13). These are self-designations of oneness by the Father and the Son. "I and the Father are one" (John 10:30).

God is the beginning and the end. God holds all time in an eternal now. The spring of the water of life is a preview of the Holy Spirit (22:1–2). These who overcome enjoy a special relationship as God's children (Ephesians 1:3–5). The saints who overcome shall reign in the kingdom of God (20:4). They experience the first resurrection, and over them, the second death has no power (20:6).

8

But those deceived by the father of lies (John 8:44) suffer the second death (20:6, 14, 21:8) with its lake of fire. Again, it must be asked if they are truly tormented forever and ever (20:10)? This needs still to be addressed farther, and the Greek can at times mean for a very long time. In the study of Revelation, it is easy to forget the symbolic nature of the book. This includes even the phrase, forever and ever, for this too is symbolic. Forever and ever is not about our time, but God's time, not this age, but the age to come, where all bets are off. Except for the grace of God revealed in the Lamb, none of us would be able to stand. How can true justice lump all together in a fiery flame? We trust our God is just, every time, and that punishment always fits the crime.

As fire may symbolize the chastisement of God's love, severe, there is hope still, that in Christ all will be made alive. That all does mean all. Christ is raised, and then those who are Christ's at his coming are raised (1 Corinthians 15:23). Then comes the end (1 Corinthians 15:24). The last enemy, death, is abolished (1 Corinthians 15:26). All things are put under Christ's rule (1 Corinthians 15:27) until finally that God may be all in all (1 Corinthians 15:28). This sequence (1 Corinthians 15:20–28) complements the scenes of Revelation 19:11–22:6. See also Colossians 1:13–20.

Scene Six: The Bride-City, Her Glory (21:9–14)

Then one of the seven angels with the seven bowls full of the seven last plagues came and spoke with me, saying, "Come here, I will show you the bride, the wife of the Lamb." And he carried me away in the Spirit to a great high mountain, and showed me the holy city,

Jerusalem, coming down out of heaven from God, with the glory of God.

Its brilliance is like a very costly stone, like a stone of crystal-clear jasper. It has a great high wall, with twelve gates, and at the gates twelve angels; and names were written, which are the names of the twelve tribes of the sons of Israel. There are three gates on the east and three gates on the north and three gates on the south and three gates on the west. And the wall of the city has twelve foundation stones, and on them are the twelve names of the twelve apostles of the Lamb.

9–14

The bride is contrasted with the woman in scarlet (17–18). The bride is introduced (21:9) in the same way as the latter's judgment had been introduced (17:1). John is previously carried in the Spirit into a wilderness (17:3) to see the great city (Babylon), as the bowl judgments come to an end (17:1). This vision includes seven parts and relies on Ezekiel 40–48.[31] The seven parts will be examined in turn. In the first part of the vision (9–10), John is carried in the Spirit to a great high mountain (Ezekiel 40:2) to see the bride, the holy city (Jerusalem).

In this second part of the vision (11–14), the city descends with God's glory (God's presence). God is coming to earth. This coming of the city is a companion scene to the coming of the rider on the white horse (19:11–16). These scenes of act VII all represent a collage of events in the age to come. Ancient cities depended on the size of their walls for safety. The city's great high wall is a symbol of security and peace (shalom). The walls bear the names of the twelve tribes (Ezekiel 48:31–34) and the names of the twelve apostles on its foundation stones. Twelve plus twelve, twenty-four, stands for the people of God, the Old and the New, united in true joy and harmony.

Scene Six: The Bride-City, Her Dimensions (21:15–21)

The one who spoke with me had a gold measuring rod to measure the city, and its gates and its walls. The city is laid out as a square, and its length is as great as the width; and he measured the city with the rod, twelve thousand stadia; its length and width and height are equal. And he measured its wall, a hundred and forty-four cubits, according to human measurements, which are also angelic measurements.

The material of the wall was jasper; and the city was pure gold, like clear glass. The foundations of the city wall are adorned with every kind of precious stone. The first foundation stone was jasper; the second, sapphire; the third, chalcedony; the fourth, emerald: the fifth, sardonyx; the sixth, sardius; the seventh, chrysolite; the eighth, beryl; the ninth, topaz; the tenth, chrysoprase; the eleventh, jacinth; the twelfth, amethyst. And the twelve gates are twelve pearls; each one of the gates is a single pearl. And the street of the city is pure gold, like transparent glass.

15–17

Earlier God's people are measured to determine their endurance for suffering (11:1). Now the city's dimensions are measured to show her magnificent glory. The source for the measuring is Ezekiel 40. The city's length, height, and width are equal, a perfect cube, the shape of the Holy of Holies in the tabernacle and temple (1 Kings 6:20). The earthly temples copy the heavenly glory (Hebrews 8:5; Exodus 25:40), and to earth the heavenly is coming. A Stadia, the length of a stadium, is 600 feet. 12,000 is symbolic as twelve stands for God's people. This is a big-tent city, a tabernacle with room for all from far and wide. A cubit is approximately eighteen inches; the walls measure 144 cubits. Just as twelve plus twelve represents the people of God, the same is true of twelve times twelve, 144, which symbolizes God's people, the bride of Christ.

18–21

The city symbolizes a gigantic Holy of Holies covered with pure gold (1 Kings 6:20). The great high wall is not a foreboding defense against God's enemies because there are no longer any enemies. But there are still those outside the wall. Who are they? These are the ones in the lake of fire. Jasper expresses God's glory (4:3, 21:11), and the wall's radiant glory intends to awaken a longing and a hope in those who remain on the outside looking in. The miracle of an encounter with the Most-High God is possible still.[32]

The foundation stones (Isaiah 54:11–12) model the stones of the high priest's gold breastplate (Exodus 28:15–21). Pearls are signs of great value. Jesus compares the kingdom of God to a merchant who sells all he owns in order to buy a pearl of great price (Matthew 13:45–46). No wonder a golden city with gates of pearl. But remember this is all symbolic still, and only in the age to come will we know the beauty of the Lamb.

Scene Six: The Bride-City, Her Illumination (21:22–27)

I saw no temple in it, for the Lord God, the Almighty and the Lamb are its temple. And the city has no need of the sun or the moon to shine on it, for the glory of God has illumined it, and its lamp is the Lamb. The nations will walk by its light, and the kings of the earth will bring their glory into it.

And its gates will never be closed in the daytime; and there will be no night there; and they will bring the glory and the honor of the nations into it; but nothing unclean will ever come into it, and no one who practices abomination and lying, but only those whose names are written in the Lamb's book of life.

22–26

No temple is needed. It's replaced by the Lord God and the Lamb. The vision's fifth part shows the glory and splendor of the one seated on the throne (4:1–11) and the Lamb (5:1–14). As heaven comes to earth, God's glory (Isaiah 60:19–20) and the Lamb's light are all that is needed (John 8:14). Heaven and earth join in perfect harmony, restoring the shalom of God among his creation as in the glorious garden of Eden (Genesis 3:8). This next part of the vision (24–26) shows the city's importance for the kings and nations of the earth. They are back again to walk in the light of the Lamb. The kings and their armies were not killed by the sword from the mouth of the one seated on the white horse (19:21). That battle represents the triumph of God's word over the forces of evil.

The gates are never shut. The nations will come to the light (Isaiah 60:3), all drawn by the glory of the walls of Jasper 21:18 and the open gates of pearl. It is promised all the nations will come and worship before God (15:4; Psalm 86:9). Why else are the gates open? Except in the age to come, in dim, timeless mystery (1 Corinthians 13:12), it's still possible to be drawn by the glorious, radiant beauty of the slain Lamb (1 Corinthians 15:22; Colossians 1:19–20), and to enter the city.

Now it's time yet again to revisit the Book of Life and lake of fire (20:1–15). Those in the Book of Life are the resurrected saints. They are the bride of Christ; they are the holy city with its gates open wide. Who are those who are not in the holy city? They are the ones whose names are not written in the Book of Life; they are the ones in the lake of fire. These suffered the second death.

27

The vision warns all those who are disgraced by their vile behavior and lying. The God of truth cannot allow liars to enter, only those whose names are in the Book of Life. Yet, all is by grace, and Jesus can bring liars to faith by leaving open the gates. Jesus says, "If I am lifted up from the earth, I will draw all people to myself" (John 12:32). God is still able to draw all from second death to second resurrection into the Book of Life through the city gates.

What about names written in the Book of Life? (13:8, 20:15, 21:17) Old names may be erased (3:5), and new names may be received (2:17). If an old name is not written, the new name may be there. All things are possible with God. Support for universal salvation can be found in scripture, including Revelation. This study only raises that possibility, but a careful and thoughtful defense of universal salvation is beyond the purpose of this book. One of the best books on the subject is in the bibliography.[33]

Scene Seven: The Holy Spirit, the River of Life (22:1-5)

Then he showed me a river of the water of life, clear as crystal, coming from the throne of God and of the Lamb, in the middle of its street. On either side of the river was the tree of life, bearing twelve kinds of fruit, yielding its fruit every month; and the leaves of the tree were for the healing of the nations. There was no longer any curse; and the throne of God and of the Lamb will be in it, and his bond-servants will serve him; they will see his face, and his name will be on their foreheads. And there will no longer be any night; and they will not have need of the light of a lamp nor the light of the sun, because the Lord God will illumine them; and they will reign forever and ever.

1–2

The river of the water of life, flowing from the temple (Ezekiel 47:1), becomes a mighty river (47:5). This is like a river from the garden of Eden (Genesis 2:10) and, on either side, the Tree of Life (Genesis 2:9) yielding its fruit and leaves for healing (Ezekiel 47:12). There is a river that makes glad the city of God (Psalm 46:4). Everyone who thirsts come to the waters (Isaiah 55:1). The Holy Spirit is the water of life flowing from the throne of God and the Lamb. (The Holy Spirit proceeds from the Father and the Son.) The Spirit is the living water, available to all who come to Jesus and drink (John 7:37–39). John sees this wondrous harmony of God's throne, the Lamb that was slain, and the flowing water of life, all together in a vision of the blessed Trinity.

3–5

In Revelation's central image, the divine throne room (4:1–5:14), God, the Lamb, and the Spirit are surrounded by twenty-four elders and four living creatures. This inner circle of priests leads all creation in worship. In the New Jerusalem, all enjoy the immediate access to the throne of God. In the earthly temple, the high priest once a year entered the Holy of Holies, wearing God's sacred name on his forehead, and no one could see God's face and live (Exodus 33:20–23). In New Jerusalem, the peoples' fervent desire to know God is realized (Psalm 17:15), and they will see God face to face and live.[34]

The last act of Revelation's great drama is finished. All the martyrs and saints, all the people of God, even those outside the city gates, may be drawn at last to God's reign of love and grace. All are now able to see face-to-face the paradise that God has prepared (1 Corinthians

2:9, 12:12). It's the garden of Eden restored. As the curtain falls on the forty-ninth scene of the drama, act VII is finished. Yet the drama is not yet over. There is still a conclusion to be reached. Don't let anyone leave the theater. Wait a little longer still.

THE EPILOGUE (22:6–21)

And he said to me, "These words are faithful and true"; and the Lord, the God of the Spirits of the prophets, sent his angel to show to his bond-servants the things which must soon take place.

"**And look, I am coming quickly**. Blessed is the one who keeps the words of the prophesy of this book."

I, John, am the one who heard and saw these things. And when I heard and saw, I fell to worship at the feet of the angel who showed me these things. But he said to me, "Do not do that. I am a fellow servant of yours and of your brothers and sisters, the prophets, and with those who keep the words of this book.

Then he said to me, "Do not seal up the words of the prophecy of this book, for the time is near. Let the evil doer still do evil, and the impure still be impure, and the righteous still do right, and the holy still be holy.

Look, I am coming quickly, and my reward is with me to repay all according to what they have done. I am the Alpha and the Omega, the first and the last, the beginning and the end."

Blessed are those who wash their robes, so they may have the right to the tree of life, and may enter by the gates into the city. Outside are the dogs and the sorcerers and the immoral persons and the murderers and the idolaters and everyone loves and practices lying.

"I, Jesus have sent my angel to testify to you for the churches of these things. I am the root and the descendant of David, the bright morning star."

> The Spirit and the Bride say, "Come."
> And let the one who hears say, "Come."
> And let the one who is thirsty come.
> Let the one who desires take the water of life without cost.

I testify to everyone who hears the words of the prophecy of this book: If anyone adds to them, God will add to him the plagues that are written in this book. And if anyone takes away from the words of the book of this prophecy, God will take away that person's share in the Tree of Life and Holy City, which are written in this book.

He who testifies to these things says, **"Yes, I am coming quickly."**

Amen, Come, Lord Jesus. The grace of the Lord Jesus be with you all. Amen.

6-9

The angel from verse 5 continues to speak. God's message was given to Jesus to show his bond-servants, and the message was sent through John (1:1). This introduces Jesus who speaks in verse seven. Then John speaks in verse 8 and the angel again in verse 9. There are obvious similarities between the epilogue and prologue. Angels address John in each. There is the emphasis on "the things which must soon take place" (1:1). There is a similar blessing on "the one who keep the words of the prophecy" (1:3). And John falling at the feet of the angel to worship him is almost identical to an earlier incident (19:10).

10–13

The time is late but not too late. Summaries of the warnings and joys are given.[35] The plagues, when understood as warnings for this age, are designed to shock people to change their ways. These include acts III, V, and VI. A farther word must be added here because the greatest motivation is fear. More than love or grace, fear motivates humans.

As we embrace the Lamb so dear, may we let go of all our fear (1 John 4:18). There are also the pictures of joy and salvation, which are designed to prod those who straddle the fence to keep on keeping on in their witness, no matter the cost. Other similarities with the prologue, include "the time is near" (1:3), emphasizing the opportunity for change is at hand. The self-declaration of Christ, "I am the Alpha and the Omega," matches the self-declaration of God (1:8) in the prologue and balances two statements of Christ (1:17, 22:13) and two statements of God (1:8, 22:16). The most significant part of the epilogue are Jesus's words, "I am coming quickly" (22:7, 12, 20). This will we examine in-depth later.

14–15

New Jerusalem is a recreation of the garden of Eden, as the new heaven and earth are the redemption of God's entire creation. Those who may enter the garden city have washed their robes clean with the Lamb's blood (7:14), meaning they have been willing to suffer for him and have followed the Lamb wherever he goes (14:4). Ancient societies placed in their temples the images of their gods. God created heaven and earth as a temple and placed humans made in his image in the garden, in the inner sanctum of God's magnificent heaven-and-earth temple (Genesis 1:27, 2:8).

In the garden, sin kept humans from the tree of life (Genesis 2:9, 3:22). God did more than close the garden and put up a keep-out sign (Genesis 3:24). Sin is kept outside the gates (21:8). Those banned from the city follow in the disgrace of the unholy trinity, of which Satan is liar-in-chief. Lying is a gateway to other crimes. A nation led by a liar cannot stand in the judgment (Psalm 1).

16–17

Jesus validates the message God sent through him to the angel to give to John (1:1, 22:6). He is the root of David, the Messianic king (5:5; Isaiah 11:1, 10). "A star shall come forth from Jacob" (Numbers 24:17). The star is a familiar symbol in Jewish writings for the expected Davidic king.

The Spirit and the bride extend the gracious invitation to drink of the water of life. This takes the drama back to its last two scenes. Scene six of act VII is the scene of the bride, the Holy City. And scene seven is the scene of the Spirit, the river of life. The Spirit and the church (Acts 2:1–4) echo Jesus's gracious invitation to come and drink from the life-giving stream (John 7:37). It harkens back to Isaiah's earlier invitation (Isaiah 55:1). The Spirit and the church voice Christ's invitation to the dramatic conclusion of John's masterly, magnificent Revelation drama, the fiftieth scene. Yes, I am coming quickly. Christ is coming as the fiftieth scene, the Jubilee!

18-21

John closes with a final warning, which he sees as Christ's warning not to add or subtract from the message. Christ is the one who is faithful and true, who gives his testimony, "Yes, I am coming quickly," for the third time. Christ himself is coming as the fiftieth and concluding scene in the drama. In summary, Revelation is written in the context of a specific worldview that divides time into this age and the age to come. Yet God lives in the eternal now, in another dimension beyond all time and space. Scientists now speak of the possibly of other dimensions. Think of heaven as another dimension not far away, but very close, where God sees all time at once (Psalm 90:4). This means God is always near and Christ is always coming quickly. Therefore, Christ calls us to live each day, as if he is knocking at the door (3:20). Because he is!

Christ Our Jubilee

This drama has seven acts of seven scenes, forty-nine in all. A closer look at the number seven can aid our understanding of Revelation's message. Seven is first mentioned with the seven days of creation and the tradition of the Sabbath day, a day of rest (Genesis 1:1–2:3). The Israelites were slaves in Egypt; slaves never have a day off. The Sabbath is a revolutionary idea, a day for worship and a day for rest (a holy day). The seventh scene in each act of Revelation is a Sabbath scene.

1. Scene seven of the seven churches: Jesus's invitation to commune with him (3:20)
2. Scene seven of the seven seals: A call to silent worship (8:1)
3. Scene seven of the seven trumpets: A scene of worship before the throne of God (11:15–16)
4. Scene seven of the seven insights: All the nations will come and worship before the throne of God (15:4)
5. Scene seven of the seven bowls: A loud voice announces, "It is done" (16:17), an echo of Genesis 2:2 as God rests from creating
6. Scene seven of the seven words of justice: The four living creatures and twenty-four elders fall before God in worship (19:4)
7. Scene seven of the seven visions of Christ's coming: A vision of God's people serving (worshiping) the Holy Trinity (22:1–5)

The Sabbath laid the foundation for Jewish holy days and annual festivals. Noteworthy is the festival of weeks (Leviticus 23:8–16). Known as Pentecost, it's the fiftieth day after seven Sabbaths. A first fruits offering was given to God on the first day of the fifty; the spring harvest began after the fiftieth day. Jesus's resurrection occurred on the festival of first fruits. The Holy Spirit came upon Jesus's disciples on the fiftieth day, the Day of Pentecost, and the harvest of new believers began (Acts 2).

The seventh Jewish month has three festivals. The Festival of Trumpets (Leviticus 23:23–24; Numbers 29:1–6) came the first day of the month. It began ten days of repentance and consecration to prepare for the holiest day, the Day of Atonement (Leviticus 16:8–34, 23:27–32). To atone means to cover. The ritual sacrifices prescribed for the Day of Atonement are to cover the people's sins and achieve reconciliation with God. Jesus secured atonement once and for all; covered are sins and reconciled us to God (Hebrews 9:1–14).

Following the Day of Atonement, the Festival of Booths began on the fifteenth day of the seventh month. The first and last days of the eight-day festival were Sabbath days. This festival commemorated the journey of the people of Israel living in tents during their wilderness journey (Leviticus 23:42–43). It marked the beginning of the fall harvest season and was also known as the Festival of Ingathering (Exodus 34:22). On the last day of this festival, Jesus spoke about the coming Holy Spirit as like the rivers of water flowing from the hearts of believers (John 7:37–39).

A Sabbath year came every seven years (Leviticus 25:1–7). Fields were not planted, and the land rested. The year of Jubilee occurred after seven Sabbath years (Leviticus 25:8–17). On the Day of Atonement, in the forty-ninth year, the trumpet sounded to announce the Jubilee year. The original owners had leased, mortgaged, or lost land returned to them. Debts were forgiven. Slaves, indentured servants, and prisoners were set free.

Early in his ministry, Jesus came to his hometown synagogue in Nazareth and read from Isaiah 61:1–2, a scripture announcing freedom for the captives and oppressed and proclaiming the year of the Lord's favor, the year of Jubilee. Jesus announces he is that fulfillment of the Jubilee year! (Luke 4:14–19).

On one hand, the grand Revelation drama awaits completion with the coming of Jesus, the slain and standing Lamb who is the embodiment of the year of Jubilee. But on the other hand, he is already coming quickly and always knocking at the door (3:20). Christ comes quickly every day, as scene fifty of the Revelation drama, a scene to be lived each day. Every day Christ is knocking; he is still knocking. He is our Jubilee; will we open the door?

Revelation for Today

This Revelation drama continues to be of immense value for today's church. The church music gleaned from Revelation has been a treasure chest for the church's worship. This drama sounds its urgent call to

- resist the evil around and within us all;
- unceasingly witness to the good news and patiently listen to each other's views;
- humbly walk with Jesus along the way we go, no matter what we think we know
- and taking it slow down the path of grace
- to encourage others as we run the race;
- and make it our goal in this life we live
- the blessed Trinity, our worship, to give:

To give thanks for faith, hope, and love from our gracious father above,
and the Spirit who comes on the wings of a dove,
and the Lamb of God, whose blood stains the sod.

The Lamb's blood is shed for all—black or white or small or tall. We are created as one human family to worship the Lamb who is all-worthy. God is the One who makes all things new, and God gives us many tasks to do: to care for God's creation and work for legislation to combat climate change and keep temperatures within range. And resist the beast that feeds on lies and all the latest conspiracies that keep us from our sacred duty to preserve all God's created beauty.

Worthy is the Lamb who provides living water for the thirsty, the finest bread for the hungry, and blessed rest for the weary. Jesus has no hands but our hands, and we need always to take a stand. Keep on keeping on to do your best and then to God leave all the rest. Worthy is the Lamb! He is knocking! Please open the door!

BIBLIOGRAPHY

Aulen, Gustaf. *Christus Victor: An historical study of the three main types of the idea of the Atonement.* London: S.P.C.K., 1970.

Barclay, William. *The Revelation of John, Volume 1 and 2: The Daily Study Bible Series.* Philadelphia: The Westminster Press, 1960.

Bauckham, Richard. *The Theology of the Book of Revelation: New Testament Theology.* United Kingdom: Cambridge University Press, 1993.

Beale, G. K. & Campbell, David H. *Revelation: A Shorter Commentary.* Grand Rapids, Mich.: William B, Eerdsmans Publishing Co., 2015.

Blount, Brian K. *Revelation: A Commentary: The New Testament Library.* Louisville: Westminster John Knox Press, 2009.

———. *Can I Get A Witness? Reading Revelation through African American Culture.* Louisville: Westminster John Knox Press, 2005.

Bowman, John Wick. *The Drama of the Book of Revelation.* Philadelphia: The Westminster Press, 1955.

———. *The Interpreter's Dictionary of the Bible, Volume 4, Book of Revelation.* New York: Abingdon Press, 1962.

Boyd, Gregory A. *God at War: The Bible & Spiritual Conflict.* Downers Grove, Ill.: Inter Varsity Press, 1997.

Campbell, R. Dennis. *He Shall Reign: The Meaning and Message of the Book of Revelation.* Baltimore: Publish America, 2004.

Daniels, C. Wess. *Resisting Empire: The Book of Revelation as Resistance.* Newberg, Ore.: Barclay Press, Inc., 2019.

Fiorenza, Elisabeth S. *Revelation: Proclamation Commentaries; The New Testament Witnesses for Preaching.* Philadelphia: Fortress Press, 1977.

———. *The Book of Revelation: Justice and Judgment. Second Addition.* Minneapolis: Fortress Press, 1998

MacDonald, Gregory, *The Evangelical Universalist: Second Edition.* Eugene, Ore.: Cascade Books, 2012.

Middleton, J. Richard, *A New Heaven and a New Earth: Reclaiming Biblical Eschatology.* Grand Rapids, Mich.: Baker Academic, 2014.

Mounce, Robert H. *The Book of Revelation: The New International Commentary.* Grand Rapids, Mich.: Wm. B. Eerdsmans Publishing, 1977.

Peterson, Eugene H. *Reversed Thunder: The Revelation of John & the Praying Imagination.* New York: HarperCollins Publishers, 1988.

Rissi, Mathias. *The Future of the World: Exegetical Study of Revelation 19.11-22.15, Studies in Biblical Theology.* London: SCM Press LTD, 1972.

———. *Time and History: A Study on the Revelation, translated by Gordon C. Winsor*. Richmond, Va.: John Knox Press, 1966.

Rossing, Barbara R. *The Rapture Exposed: The Message of Hope in the Book of Revelation*. United Kingdom: Westview Press, Oxford, 2004.

Smalley, Stephen S. *The Revelation to John: A Commentary on the Greek Text of the Apocalypse*. Downers Grove, Ill.: InterVarsity Press, 2005.

———. *Thunder and Love: John's Revelation and John's Community*. Eugene, Ore.: Wipf & Stock Publishers, 1994.

Storms, Sam. *Kingdom Come, The Amillennial Alternative*. Scotland: Mentor, Christian Focus Publications Ltd, 2013.

Wilcock, Michael *The Message of Revelation: I Saw Heaven Opened*. Nottingham: Inter-Varsity Press, 1975.

Wright, N, T. *Surprised by Hope, Rethinking Heaven, the Resurrection, & the Mission of the Church*. New York: Harper Collins Publishers, 2008.

———. *Revelation for Everyone: New Testament for Everyone*. Louisville: Westminster John Knox Press, 2011.

———. *The Day the Revolution Began: Reconsidering the Meaning of Jesus's Crucifixion*. New York: Harper Collins Publishers, 2016.

Zuendel, Friedrich. *The Awakening: One Man's Battle with Darkness*. Farmington, Penn.: The Plow Publishing House, 1999.

ENDNOTES

1   Matthias Rissi, *The Future of the World: Studies in Biblical Theology, Second Series* (London: SCM Press LTD, 1972), 3.

2   Stephen S. Smalley, *Thunder and Love: John's Revelation and John's Community* (Eugene, Ore.: Wipf & Stock Publishers, 1994), 49–50.

3   John Wick Bowman, *The Drama of the Book of Revelation* (Philadelphia: The Westminster Press, 1955).

4   Richard Bauckham, *The Theology of the Book of Revelation: New Testament Theology* (United Kingdom: Cambridge University Press, 1993), 17.

5   Brian K. Blount, *Revelation: A Commentary: The New Testament Library* (Louisville: Westminster John Knox Press, 2009), 41–42.

6   N. T. Wright, *Revelation for Everyone: New Testament for Everyone* (Louisville: Westminster John Knox Press, 2011), 10-39, for more about the cities of the seven churches.

7   Robert H. Mounce, *The Book of Revelation: The New International Commentary* (Grand Rapids, Mich.: Wm. B. Eerdsmans Publishing, 1977), 83-130, for more about the cities of the seven churches.

8   Bauckham, 80.

9   Ibid., 81.

10 Ibid., 86–87.

11 Ibid., 87.

12 Ibid., 84

13 Gregory A. Boyd, *God at War: The Bible and Spiritual Conflict* (Downers Grove, Ill.: Inter Varsity Press, 1997).

14 Bauckham, 84.

15 Ibid., 94–96.

16 Gregory MacDonald, *The Evangelical Universalist* (Eugene, Ore.: Cascade Books, 2012), 113.

17 Ibid., 109.

18 Ibid., 127.

19 Blount, *Revelation: A Commentary*, 307.

20 Wright, 168.

21 Rissi, 19.

22 Blount, 354.

23 Rissi, 29–30.

24 R. Dennis Campbell, *He Shall Reign: The Meaning and Message of the Book of Revelation* (Baltimore: Publish America, 2004).

25 Barbara R. Rossing, *The Rapture Exposed: The Message of Hope in the Book of Revelation* (United Kingdom: Westview Press, Oxford, 2004).

26 Sam Storms, *Kingdom Come: The Amillennial Alterative* (Scotland: Mentor, Christian Focus Publications Ltd, 2013).

27 Bauckham, 106–107.

28 Rissi, 35–36.

29 Mattias Rissi, *Time and History: A Study on the Revelation* (Richmond, Vir.: John Knox Press, 1966), 123–125.

30 Blount, 378.

31 Rissi, *The Future of the World*, 60.

32 Rissi, 71.

33 MacDonald, *The Evangelical Universalist*.

34 Bauckham, 142.

35 Blount, 406.

9 781664 210844